Take a Walk in My Shoes

---- ❁ ----

Take a Walk in My Shoes

B. J. Parker

Archway Publishing books may be ordered
through booksellers or by contacting:

Archway Publishing
1663 Liberty Drive
Bloomington, IN 47403
www.archwaypublishing.com
1-(888)-242-5904

ISBN: 978-1-4808-0497-5 (sc)
ISBN: 978-1-4808-0498-2 (e)

Library of Congress Control Number: 2013958353

Printed in the United States of America

Archway Publishing rev. date: 1/23/2014

Dedication

———— ✿ ————

To those victims who have not found their way back, those who are facing difficulties every day in an attempt to heal, and the victims who have taken the steps to find their way.

Put your feet in my shoes and we will walk together.

Prologue

———————— ❁ ————————

*A*s I lay here with this man, the one who is supposed to protect his teenage daughter above all else, I try to remember how this came to be our frequent practice. This room has always been strictly forbidden, yet I lay in their marital bed. My body responds to his touch. What is wrong with me? No matter how hard I try to dismiss what happens, my mind sways from feelings of evil to those of pleasure. This is wrong. I hate myself—I am abominable and disgusting.

In one swift motion I am off the bed. I bend over, quickly pick my panties off the floor, and walk towards the door. I don't want to look at him. Physical and emotional feelings overwhelm; I have betrayed my mom and he has betrayed us both. I feel a churning deep in the pit of my stomach, the purge building. My body shakes as if I had been outside on a winter day without a coat and my knees want to fold underneath me. Two more steps will make 14, and that's how many it takes until I am in the bathroom, safe. For now. I have to wash away the evil veil that encases me. It feels tight and stifling. I force myself to take a breath of air. My hands shake uncontrollably as I turn on the faucet. I raise my head; the reflection in the mirror reveals an ugly, horrible face that hides revolting secrets. My eyes are red, filled with tears. My face looks pale. With each encounter I beg him to stop, but my pleading falls upon deaf ears.

❁

Hello. My name is Bonnie and I am a sexual assault victim.

The human brain is a fascinating entity, made up of different lobes, cells, chemicals, and transmitters that control the slightest movements of the body. It holds vast amounts of information, allowing humans to express or suppress emotions. The psyche has the ability to recall the smallest of details: a specific fragrance, fabric, picture, song or location can bring back cherished memories or those that reignite grief, sorrow, and intense fear. Victims of traumatic experiences often place painful memoirs in imaginary boxes, closed and bound tightly. These boxes are not adorned with jewels, fancy bows, or tags, nor are they brightly colored. Mine is dark and very well constructed. It is comparable to that of a mausoleum or tomb—*impermeable*. Its sole purpose has been to hold the anguish I endured at the hands of a man I called "Dad." It has sat undisturbed for over forty years.

In 2010, I began thinking about the box from time to time, imagining its contents. *Certainly it must be bursting at the seams by now.* Initially, I wasn't the least bit curious about its collection, although I knew in my mind's eye it had to be quite a stash. Occasionally, fleeting thoughts of the box darted through my mind, grating on me like nails across a chalkboard. These thoughts soon became overpowering and I felt compelled to open the box. As soon as I looked for it, the box was right there, hanging over me like a storm cloud ready to gush. *NO!* I heard my mind scream. *Do not open it; there is simply no need to do it. What is the point? There's no point.* Sometimes, I wanted to shout at the box: *LEAVE ME ALONE!*

The impulse did not let up. One day, I found myself seriously considering the possibility a more palatable approach: What if I could somehow gently bring the box out into the light? I could see it clearly in my mind's eye: charred black with scaly, burnt wood. Rusty hinges. Countless yards of dirty twine binding my memories and emotions. Slowly, I reached to pull the box forward, inch by inch, until it teetered on the edge of imagination, threatening my reality.

Why now, Bonnie? Why, after all these years, would you even consider lifting the lid? Because it's time to heal. Take the voyage. Walk the paths. Laugh, cry, feel the anger and hatred. In the end, the passage may lead you to your aspirations: You can thrive! It's time to help yourself. Open it! Examine one thing at a time, starting at the beginning…

Chapter One

———— ❀ ————

I was born in 1958. My mother's name is Orlena. My earliest child-hood memories are of preschool age at which time my mother was single, raising my sister Anne, who was seven years my senior, and me. In 1963, our small family of three lived in what is now known as the projects in a small town in Northern Michigan. However, in the late 50's to late 60's, the apartments were far from the run down, low income housing units they are today. Originally, they were built to lodge spouses and children of men serving in the military. Years later they were purchased by individuals and used as rentals for those in the community. Many were four unit apartments, which included spacious kitchens, and a living room on the main floors, with two bedrooms and a bath on the second floors.

I remember having our milk delivered by the milkman who placed four glass bottles of milk in a square-shaped, silver, metal container that sat on the small stoop outside our door. Sometimes, my mom would get cottage cheese in colorful metal glasses, and on special occasions she would treat my sister and me to one bottle of chocolate milk. We were always elated to see that one special jug among those of white. Life felt carefree at that time. I was a normal kid playing with my friends, riding bicycles, swinging on swing sets, and walking all over the immediate area to visit neighbors. There was no imaginary box yet. Nothing separating me from all the other children; Nothing separating me from the world.

An elderly gentleman lived at the end of our block, the first African American man I had ever seen. He was tall, thin, and very polite. He walked the streets of our neighborhood with a warm smile. My friends and I gathered daily on his front porch and he placed a cookie on each eager, outstretched hand. We sat and talked with him for hours. One day, I asked him why his skin was so dark and he replied with a smile and a gentle voice, "I spent too much time in the Florida sun." I didn't understand his answer but it was a response and that was all I needed. Ahh, the age of true innocence.

Saturdays in our apartment were always set-aside for household chores. I don't recall having specific duties, but I reminisce about the music. Mom placed a stack of 45's on the turntable and we danced and sang while sweeping the floors, dusting furniture, and shaking throw rugs outside. We twisted to Chubby Checker, sang along with Patsy Cline, and even chimed in with Dion, The Drifters, and Roy Orbison. My mom helped me appreciate everything from the Big Band Era, orchestra compositions, to modern day pop. Even today, the first thing I turn on every morning is my radio.

In 1963, my mother met Derrick. He was divorced and owned his own construction business. I don't remember the first time we met or the first time he came into our apartment. I don't even recall Mom going out on dates with him. But one year later, in 1964, Mom and Derrick married in a double ceremony with another couple who were long time friends. I do remember my mom's wedding dress, though, hand-sewn from the most beautiful lavender fabric. Mom had carefully cut the pieces of delicate satin and lace, pinning and sewing relentlessly until the big day finally arrived. The hem fell perfectly just below her knees and matching lavender heels made her ensemble gorgeous.

Derrick adopted me in 1965 and I vaguely recall making trips to a lawyer's office. Shortly after, we moved into a house in the country with an elementary school directly across the street. I attended only a portion of kindergarten there but can still see clearly the beautiful hard wood floors of that schoolhouse. Comfort seemed so easy to come by, then; so delightfully simple. My struggles came few and far between: One Easter Sunday, my sister and I sat on the floor across from one another, methodically counting each piece of candy in our baskets. Her basket contained one portion more than mine. I cried and cried and mom never made that mistake again!

Our next house is the one that remains in my mind; every nook and cranny. There were two bedrooms on the main floor, a bathroom, an open kitchen with a dining area, and a living room. The basement stairs were just off the dining area—totaling 13 steps to get down to the dark, untended place. That level contained a small bedroom with an adjacent laundry chute. I also recall a laundry and recreation room. The laundry chute truly frightened me. I felt convinced a stranger lay in wait in the small room ready to grab me whenever I fell asleep. I never slept with my legs uncovered either, just in case the stranger crept about or hid underneath my bed. One night, I even moved my bookshelf in front of the door in my sleep!

Our backyard was large, fenced in, and had a shed at the farthest end of the property and a very old weeping willow. I disliked that tree immensely, mainly due to the beetles that broke free from their shells, leaving them hanging securely to the tree. They looked like post-apocalyptic skeletons following an invasion. To this day, beetles still give me the heebie-jeebies.

Our countryside neighborhood felt nice. Lawns were well manicured, filled with beautiful trees and gardens. I always thought ours was the best, with two magnificent white birch trees in the front yard. Mom had numerous flower beds full of color, each blooming at various times in the spring and summer. They looked picturesque, deserving a full-page photo in a top notch gardening magazine. There were rose beds bathed with yellow, pink, red, and white blossoms, each with their own unique, sweet fragrance. The Hibiscus flowered in pink blooms, its petals larger than my hand and stalks as tall as my sister.

Our neighborhood was filled with other families also living in modest homes and everyone knew each other. Area children gathered to play outside, going in for lunch and dinner. My play friend was Terry; she lived 3 doors down on the same side of the street. We spent hours in her driveway with our plastic horses, making them appear to run through dirt and rear up on their hind legs. We often constructed corrals from small sticks we picked up in the yard. We whinnied and pounded their plastic hooves as our horses galloped into the sunset. No matter what, my mom's steadfast rule was for me to be home when the streetlights came on. I used to think there was a man whose only job was to flip a switch for those street lights, illuminating the countryside for miles and sending dozens and dozens of children home to their mothers.

❀

Looking back, I had a lot of questions for my mom. I used to peel potatoes for dinner while she prepared the meat and veggies. I wanted to learn about cooking and gardening—how something as small as a seed could grow into something big enough to fit into my palm, then onto my plate, and eventually fill my belly. I usually had a lot more potato attached to the peel than was necessary, and Mom used to coach me: "Bonnie, you should be able to read the newspaper through that peel." I'm sure she tired of showing me over and over how to peel a potato, and certainly felt relieved when I mastered the technique.

There were a few things, though, I felt certain I knew more about than Mom and one of those was chewing gum. I could get a good week's worth of chewing out of just one stick. I frequently asked Mom to chew gum with me, but she always said no.

One day on our way to get groceries, I asked her again: "Mom, you want a piece of bubble gum?"

"No," she said, just like hundreds of other times.

Displeased I replied, "You never want to do anything with me mom."

"Fine- give me the damn gum" she snapped.

I felt excited as I ripped off the cartoon wrapper and handed her the pink stick. She put it in her mouth and worked it around, trying to soften it up. She chewed for a few minutes and I couldn't help but notice her struggle. We pulled into the store parking lot and Mom wasted no time selecting her parking space. Mid-day on a Saturday and, as usual, the lot looked packed.

I stared at my mother's face as she fumbled with the gob of gum. Finally, she put two fingers into her mouth, all the way toward the back, and gripped. I couldn't take my eyes off her and, in an instant, she yanked as hard as she could and her top denture came out, bubble gum securely attached. Mom and I laughed and laughed, tears streaming down our faces.

Another memorable trip to the grocery store happened several years later, when I was ten or eleven years old. A well-known cereal company had offered packets of tomato seeds in specially marked boxes of cereal. I watched the commercial over and over, telling Mom how badly I wanted to grow those tomatoes. The next time she went grocery shopping, I tagged along. To her credit, Mom tried to talk me out of it. "The seeds probably won't grow" she explained, but I was not convinced.

"You will eat this cereal Bonnie, and I mean it!" she declared as she set the box in our grocery cart. "Every. Single. Bit of it!"

Indeed I ate the cereal and it was not at all to my liking. But when I finally found the seed packet hidden at the bottom, I leapt from the table as though we had won a brand new car.

"Oh please, please, *please* let me plant these tomato seeds Mom" I begged.

Soon after, she showed me my own garden spot next to the house and I carefully planted every single, teeny, tiny seed in the pack. Then I watered them. And waited. And waited. And waited. I checked them every morning and again at night, hoping to see *something* peeking out of the ground.

Several weeks later, tiny, green sprouts emerged through the dark, brown dirt. I ran as fast as I could into the house.

"Mom, guess what!?"

She looked at me as if I had lost my mind.

"Mom you got to come see! They are growing Mom! Get your shoes—c'mon— *HURRY!*"

Mom obliged and followed me to the garden spot where she couldn't believe her eyes. The ground was peppered with tiny shoots. I couldn't have been happier. We wound up with more beefsteak tomatoes that year than our family could eat. Even after Mom canned dozens of them, we handed out bushels to the neighbors. Our neighbors delighted in my luck, and while I often felt fondly about where we lived and the beauty of having my own, little garden, inside a darker seed had been planted. One that would not bear edible fruit. The kind of seed that spun and spun, conjuring darkness around my tiny world on even the brightest of days.

Chapter Two

❀

As a youngster and into my early teens, I spent every weekend with my grandparents. Each Friday, Gram would ask me what I wanted for dinner on Saturday.

"Fried chicken, mashed potatoes, gravy, and corn," I'd say, and she would laugh.

"Aren't you getting tired of that Bon?"

"No Gram. You are a good cooker!"

And so it was, every Saturday for many years, the same dinner. I loved spending time at my grandparents' house. It felt peaceful, full of tenderness and affection. Gram taught me how to play cribbage and even how to cook—in her own way. She never used recipes. Just a "pinch" of this and a "dash" of that. We washed our hair outside in summertime using a large aluminum bowl and the garden hose. I washed Gram's hair first, and then she washed mine. At times, she rinsed mine with vinegar, insisting it helped make my blonde hair shiny.

I remember a hammock in Gram's backyard where she would lay and read. One day, a black squirrel jumped from the old box elder tree and landed right on Gram's stomach. She was startled for a moment, then said: "Well, hello One Eye." I sat on the stoop, delighting in the sun on my face, while I watched in awe as that squirrel lay on the hammock with Gram. Later, I asked why she called the squirrel one eye, and she explained the squirrel had only one eye, most likely due to an accident.

"Well, how did you get her to come to you, Gram?"

"With patience Bon. Animals, like humans need to trust, and if you're nice to them you can win them over."

My quest began; by golly I was going to try out this "patience" thing and win myself a squirrel friend! Grandpa did most of the grocery shopping and began bringing beer nuts home for me, insisting squirrels couldn't resist them. One afternoon, I noticed a very young black squirrel on the sidewalk approximately ten feet in front of me. I sat down slowly on the step, beer nuts in hand. I slid my fingers into the package ever-so quietly, picked up a single nut, and tossed it gently onto the sidewalk. It came to rest close to my intended target and I waited, sitting as still I could. Finally, the squirrel took a few careful steps, keeping her eyes on me. As quick as a whip, she grabbed the nut and ran for the tree. Within a few minutes, the squirrel returned and I tossed another beer nut, then another, and another. Eventually, the squirrel moved on and I ran in the house telling Gram what I had done.

"Gram! Gram! I did it! I used patience and fed the squirrel!"

"Wonderful" she said with a smile. "Now, you must be patient and toss the nuts a little bit closer to you. Eventually, she will eat them right out of your hand."

I named my squirrel Pee Wee because she was much smaller than the other squirrels that frequently came into the yard. Eventually, Pee Wee came to trust me and she would sit beside me on the step eating nuts from my hand. I never tried to touch her, but I remember studying her sweet face. I adored the shiny black tufts of hair on the tips of her ears. She also had bright eyes, little feet, and long whiskers on each side of her mouth. Quiet moments of connection with Pee Wee were a true blessing and provided peace and privacy in my otherwise conflicted world.

Gram also taught me a great deal about the spiritual world, wildlife, and unconditional love. I can still hear the slight scuffing noises her house slippers made when she walked across the linoleum floor in the kitchen. I know exactly where the stove and refrigerator were, and how she always kept hot, soapy dishwater in the sink, washing dishes throughout the day. To the right of the sink were three drawers. Grandma stored the toaster in the bottom drawer and cooking utensils in the top drawer. But Grandpa's transistor radio lay in the middle drawer, and that caught my attention. He kept it in a light brown leather case, beneath the wood cutting board. When I spent the night, I often placed the radio under my pillow at bedtime, turned the volume down until it was barely audible, and readily drifted off to sleep.

I also remember Gram watching hours and hours of *Murder, She Wrote*. She frequently fell asleep while reading, waking later with crooked glasses and a soft look about her face. She loved to crochet, tatt, and embroider, and she wrote beautiful poetry. Many times, she recited verses from the Bible to me, which I truly enjoyed.

Grampa had a workshop in the basement where he built the most beautiful bird feeders and shadow boxes. It was typically cold down there and Gram wouldn't let me go see his projects without a sweater. She tossed one of Grampa's sweaters over my head and I wore it like a night gown—Grampa had to have been six feet tall! Gram rolled the sleeves up half a dozen times and the bottom of the sweater draped over the top of my knees. Once downstairs, I watched him measure, mark, cut, and nail various pieces of wood together. My "job" was to hammer nails into a two by four "for practice." When I had every nail secured, he removed them and let me start all over. It didn't matter what project he worked on, I enjoyed watching him bring wood to life; always something beautiful to behold. One thing was always certain: Gram would *never* run out of birdfeeders!

During the summer, Grampa and I carried a white five gallon bucket down to the edge of the lake where thick patches of wild blackberries grew. Within minutes of picking, the container would be full and we'd carry them back to the house, dump them in the stainless steel sink, and head back for more. Gram used the fruit for jam and wine. I can easily picture in my mind the large, old-fashioned wine jugs under the basement steps. Each one had a handle large enough for one finger to fit into and they all had balloons on the top opening. As the berries fermented, the balloons got larger, and as the wine process neared maturity, the balloons deflated. Although I loved the jam, I never acquired a taste for the wine.

One summer afternoon, Grampa asked if I'd like to go fishing.

"I have a brand new cane pole to break in today," he said. "Let's go!"

"Alright!" I could hardly believe my luck.

Down to the lake we went, two poles and a tackle box in hand. When he started to load the boat I grew nervous.

"Grampa, I don't want to go out in the boat," I said. "Can't we just fish from the dock?"

He looked a little puzzled and replied, "We aren't going to catch anything from the dock Butter-Cup."

But I insisted on staying on shore and Grampa gave in, proudly handing me his brand new cane pole. It felt long and cumbersome but, with his help, I placed a night crawler on the hook and tossed it in the water at the end of the dock. It didn't go very far, however, in a matter of seconds I felt a tug on the line, and whatever I hooked put up a fight. I backed down the dock trying to get the "monster" out of the water. I pulled on the pole with all my might and Grampa rooted for me: "Don't let go! Keep pulling!" When the creature briefly surfaced, Grampa announced: "Holy mackerel, you got a big one."

He reached into the boat for his fish net and as he placed it beneath the fish, Grampa's new pole snapped in half. I had snagged a large mouth bass!

"See Grampa, I *told* you we could catch a fish from the dock," I said later.

"Gram isn't going to believe this!" he said. "Let's get this home and we can have fish for dinner!"

Fish for dinner? No! I began crying and begged Grampa not to kill the fish.

"The fish will die anyway Butter-Cup; it has to have water to breathe."

"Well, can't we put it in the birdbath Grampa? Please, please?"

As we neared the yard, Grampa looked at me, shook his head, and laid the fish in the birdbath. It was so large, its head and tail extended far beyond the circumference of the bowl, allowing only the body to be partially submerged. Needless to say, the fish died, I cried, and we had fried bass for dinner.

Full of tears or full of gratitude, these times with Gram and Grampa nourished me. These were the moments of childhood where I could forget, sometimes for days, about the secret inside of me. As I grew older, however, I worried that the world could see my wretchedness. I felt something powerful inside of me, something that could turn my world upside down at any moment. Like the lake Grampa and I fished in, I, too, carried unseen creatures. My secrets were growing, bigger than the large mouth bass I had caught. Big enough, I feared, that one day they might swallow me whole.

Chapter Three

━━━━━━━ ❁ ━━━━━━━

I always walked to and from elementary school, taking the same route each day. I remember strolling down my street, cutting across the park, then ambling over the narrow bridge covering a small stream. From there, I treaded up a steep hill and hopped onto the paved road. I often stopped at a house along the way to pick up my friend Heidi, who lived with her grandmother. She and I walked the remainder of the way together, talking and laughing.

I hated recess as I never felt I "fit in" with other kids. I felt certain people looked at me and could tell I was different, damaged. I grew timid and didn't play on the merry-go-round, jump rope, or participate in hopscotch. Instead, I headed for the swings, choosing a seat from other school mates. I remember pumping my legs so hard, the swing would loft in the air and hold me parallel with the sky for a brief moment. Elevated far above the ground, I looked at the blue and white sky and lifted my face toward the sun, all the while talking to God in my mind. If only I could jump out of the seat once the swing reached its highest point, maybe God would catch me and take me with him. My mind held a vivid picture of myself floating far above the playground, and then instantaneously, I would disappear to Heaven. Try as I might, I never got farther than the very edge of my seat on that swing.

Sometime when I was 7 years old, I remember telling Gram that my Dad was touching me.

"Touching you?" Her eyes grew wide with shock. "In what way?" she asked. "Where?"

I knew from the look on her face and the tone of her voice she felt angry. My small, shaking fingers pointed: "Down there."

Time stood still as Gram tried to wrap her mind around my words. "Have you told your mother?" she asked.

"No," I replied. My voice must have sounded shy, barely audible. *Tell my Mother! Are you crazy? He touches me in her room and I'm not allowed in there. Ever. If I tell Mom, I will be in so much trouble.*

The conversation ended just as abruptly as it began and soon Gram and I chatted, like normal. But at some point, Gram must have spoken to my mom, because suddenly Mom began taking me with her where ever she went. When she went bowling on league nights, I went too. If she went to get a pack of cigarettes, I travelled with her. Even a half-mile trek down the road to the gas station or grocery store warranted a ticket by Mom's side. I felt safe, without many cares in the world, soaking up every minute with my mom.

Sometime around 6th grade, Mom's vigilance changed. Derrick had "found religion." I remember accompanying him and my mom to various churches. He described himself as a "born again Christian." Mom must have felt she could trust Derrick again and she began leaving me at home. I felt no fear at that point, but the recommencement of Derrick's advances remains etched into my mind.

Once, I purposely left my underwear under the bed for my mom to find. I was a pre-teen and Derrick, my "Dad," couldn't keep his hands off of me. In my mind, I figured Mom would be angry that I had been in her room, then she would come to me and demand to know why and I would be able to tell her my secret. I could tell her about "down there." I could tell her about Derrick. But when the moment finally arrived, I couldn't bring myself to tell Mom the truth. I offered some believable excuse and that put an end to it. My mind had reversed the story I hoped for. Rather than imagining that telling Mom would keep me safe, I suddenly felt certain that if I told

Mom about Dad, he would grow incredibly angry. I worried that they would argue, that Mom would leave, and then she would be hurt. She loved Dad so much and she felt happy to have him in our lives. I didn't want her to be hurt by my secret.

❧

By seventh grade, my world turned upside down. I attended junior high, riding the bus to and from school each day. One warm spring afternoon, I got off at the bus stop and began the short walk home. The sun felt warm on my face. As I walked slowly up the street, I took in the beauty of the surrounding yards. I heard birds singing and I stopped at a house on the way to play with the bunnies, which I did from time to time. A family kept them in cages outside, I approached slowly to avoid scaring the bunnies. I stayed a few minutes, talking to them and watching their little, velvet noses wiggle up and down. A few houses closer to home, was where I admired the beautiful view of Mr. Williams' winding paved driveway. He kept it lined thickly on both sides with vibrant orange poppies that swayed effortlessly in the breeze, their delicate petals like thin, crinkled paper.

As I got closer to our home, I noticed Dad's truck in the driveway. *Dad must have finished a job early today*, I thought. I walked up the driveway and entered the house. Dad met me in the kitchen with a hug.

"How was school today?" he asked.

"It was O.K. How was your day?" I set my book bag on the counter and thought about an afterschool snack.

"Good," he said. He turned for the living room and I headed downstairs to my bedroom. I wanted to change out of my school clothes into a pair of shorts and a t-shirt. When I came back upstairs, I went into the living room but Dad wasn't there.

"Dad?" I called.

"In here honey," he said.

I walked toward my parents' bedroom and peered in. Dad sat on the far edge of the bed with his back towards the door. "What are you doin', Dad?"

"I want to talk to you," he said. He patted the mattress in a motion indicating he wanted me to come and sit down.

I hesitated, knowing that Mom and Dad's room was off limits. Slowly, I stepped over the threshold, walked to the bed, and sat beside him. "What's up, Dad?"

"Sweetheart, I want to talk to you for a few minutes." He placed his left hand gently on my right knee and there was a moment of silence. At first, I worried that I had done something wrong, but I quickly dismissed this. Mom was the disciplinarian in our household. "You are growing up, honey, starting to develop into a young lady. I want you to be protected when it comes to boys. All they really care about is sticking their little peckers into as many girls as they can. They don't think about getting girls pregnant."

I froze, unable to move a muscle. "Dad, I don't even have a boyfriend. I haven't even started my period!"

"Not yet," he replied. "But you will, and sometimes girls aren't able to think clearly when they get all hot and bothered. If you were to get pregnant, your mom would be hurt, angry, and very disappointed in you."

Numerous thoughts reeled through my mind: fleeting notions of confusion, nervousness, and a sense of fear that I had never experienced before. Every breath of air took effort. The bed felt as though it held invisible restraints across my body. Dad put his right hand in his pocket and pulled out a square, foil packet.

"I want you to know how to use a condom. This will keep you from getting pregnant, honey. You need to know how to put one on the right way." Without letting go of my leg, Dad unbuckled his belt, unzipped his pants, and exposed himself.

I was shocked beyond words. I couldn't believe how ugly *that thing* looked and how afraid my own Dad made me feel. He carefully opened the packet, easing the condom into his hand. He gave explicit instructions regarding the application, then took my hand and placed it around the base of his erection.

Instantly, I tried to pull my hand away. "Dad! I—I don't want to do this—please don't make me do it. Please, Dad… please!" I pleaded repeatedly.

"Honey," he said. "Have I ever hurt you?"

"No," I said. My own voice sounded a million miles away. I didn't sound like me at all.

"Okay," he whispered. "I'm not going to hurt you. I love you and I just want you to be safe."

I began crying and continued begging Dad to stop. My heart pounded and my sweaty hands shook with each beat. Tears blurred my vision. Very reluctantly, very slowly, I moved my hands and did as Dad instructed.

Once the condom was in place, Dad spoke up. "There, see…I told you I wouldn't hurt you. I love you, and there's nothing wrong with what we are doing sweetheart. I am only trying to protect you." We sat together for a few more moments until I gathered enough courage to ask permission to leave. Dad agreed, but only after stressing that I was not to tell Mom about our time together, explaining that she "wouldn't understand."

When Mom came home from work later that evening, she didn't detect anything out of the ordinary. On the outside, my act held up. But on the inside, I felt ashamed and nervous. I went to bed early that evening, silently sobbing as Dad's way of "protecting" me played over and over in my mind.

❀

While my parents' bed became a place of shame, the bottom drawer of Dad's dresser also held many secrets. There, he stored adult magazines with explicit, full page, color photos of men and women engaging in sexual acts. The magazines stayed well hidden under Dad's clothing and I'm certain my mom never knew they were there. Looking at the magazines made me feel embarrassed, my stomach tied into knots. Dad's rationale was that he needed to show me how to adequately pleasure a man. Each time he watched me turn the pages of the magazines, he quietly reminded me not to tell my mother. "She won't believe you," he would say. My list of secrets grew; my hidden box slowly constructing itself one plank at a time.

Between the magazines and Derrick's guiding hands, I learned what aspects of the penis were most sensitive, allowing the most pleasure. He liked to show me color photos in his magazines that showed a penis inside a woman, pointing out various positions, describing oral sex, and even exposing me to images of semen oozing down a penis after ejaculation. I hated looking at the photos, but looking was better than Derrick touching me, so I obliged. Eventually, looking at the pictures was not enough for him. Derrick forced me to stimulate him to the point of ejaculation, instructing me on the proper amount of squeezing and pressure so he could attain maximum enjoyment while I worked. I didn't feel fear, but I did feel indescribably uncomfortable. Shame and embarrassment wracked my body as he writhed and came against my touch.

❖

One day on my way home from school, I approached our home and realized Dad's truck wasn't in the driveway. I took a deep breath and felt my whole body relax. I entered the house with ease and went to my room to change into my play clothes. Those few moments of peace quickly turned into uneasiness when I heard Dad's truck pull in. He came in the back door and I quickly ran out the front door. I ran across the street to a neighbor's house, and climbed up the tree in their front yard as fast as my legs and arms could carry me. I knew Dad was looking for me. I watched silently from a tree limb, a bit of horror filling my gut. I knew if he found me, he would make me do those awful things to him. From my perch, I saw him open the front door and step onto the porch.

"Bonnie!" he yelled, looking from left to right.

I didn't answer. Instead, I watched him go back into the house. He must have gone out the back door, because moments later I heard him call my name again from farther away. My heart was pounding in my ears and I felt very nervous. Soon, I saw Dad sit in his chair in the living room and gaze out the picture window. I remained as still as I could, the rough bark of the tree limb pressing into my arms and legs. Eventually, he stood up and moved toward the kitchen, at the back of our house. I began easing down the tree, a little at a time, coming to rest on the lowest limb. In a flash, Dad spotted me. He moved swiftly to the screen door and opened it.

"Bonnie, it's time for you to come home," he called.

I refused to answer.

"Bonnie—I said it's time to *come home!*" His voice sounded stern.

"I'm *not* coming home!" I shouted defiantly.

"Well" he said, "you better have a good excuse when your mother gets here."

I thought about those few moments of peace I had felt when I thought I had the house to myself. I felt enraged that my own Dad could take that away from me. That he could use me for these dirty acts when, instead, I should be able to relax and play like a normal child. I conjured my strongest, most disobedient tone, I shouted back across the street: "NO! *You* better have a good excuse when my mom comes home!"

Dad closed the screen door and sat back down in his chair. A wave of terror came over me. What had I done? Now I felt even more scared than before. I lowered myself to the ground and walked across the street, defeated. I crossed the front yard, moved up the steps, and stepped into the house. Dad did not look up when I entered. He refused to even say a word, which worried me beyond belief. I quickly retreated to my room. He followed me and offered a quick flash of punishment—the first and only time he ever spanked me.

Mom came home later that evening and I knew she and Dad

were talking in the kitchen. Then, I heard Mom come down the basement steps. As she entered my room, I saw the belt in her hand.

"Did your Dad tell you to come home?" she asked.

"Yes." My palms began to sweat. I could not imagine a way out of this.

"Why didn't you do as you were told?"

"Because I didn't want to," I responded. It was the truth; but not the whole truth. How could I ever let my mother down? How could I tell her something that she didn't want to hear—something that would ruin our family? I couldn't. Mom whipped me for disobeying Dad and that was the day I refused to cry. The lashing hurt more than words can describe, but I would *not* cry. When Mom finally stopped, she looked at me quizzically, and left my room. I cried once I knew she was out of range, and could think only one thing: *Why? Why didn't you tell her?*

❧

By the time I turned fourteen, Dad began performing oral sex on me. At first, I felt immense hatred for him and a sense of overwhelming humiliation towards myself. My disgust never deterred his sickening actions. Eventually, there came a time in which my body reacted to his urgings and I reached orgasm. I could not understand how my body could betray me like this when I truly loathed what my father did to me. I felt so disillusioned with myself. Years later, I would learn that this response was not uncommon for victims of sexual abuse. Physiologically and psychologically, the body and mind develop coping mechanisms for traumatic experiences. Nearing the height of puberty, and with little to no guidance about my own development as a young woman, I was a slave to my body's responses. Right or wrong, abusive or otherwise, I could not turn off the mechanisms of pleasure. The feeling and the word took on new meaning to me: pleasure was shameful; pleasure was wrong; pleasure was my darkest, dirtiest secret ever.

It wasn't long before Dad insisted that I pleasure him orally as well. The act was repulsive and degrading, but a switch in me had been flipped. Trapped between an abusive father and an unknowing mother, torn about disappointing my family and turning the world of right and wrong upside, down, I obliged his every request. I learned quickly and performed the acts without emotion.

Chapter Four

———— ❀ ————

I sought to find my voice in other areas of my life. I had been silenced in my own home, my own family, but I could declare an identity elsewhere and I did this by rebelling. I skipped school, smoked cigarettes, and watched my once-good grades fall below average. It was somehow empowering to witness a direct and clean replay of cause and effect. Where the actions between my father and I did not make any sense, breaking a rule in school or in public society had immediate and seemingly clean-cut consequences. Out there, the world made sense, even if it was a world I bucked against. Out there, at least one plus one equaled two, and missed classes equaled failing grades. The logic of it felt comforting, although I may not have been able to describe it that way at the time. I charged forth on the only path I could make sense of.

The only place I found comfort was Gram's house, so I frequently pretended I felt sick on school days. I entered the school, headed for the office, told the principle I was ill, and then called my grandmother. She arranged for a cab and we spent the day playing cribbage or talking. As the school day came to a close, I returned to campus by cab, got on the bus, and went home just like any other day. In time, my mom made the connection, but misinterpreted my radical behavior; she forbade me from seeing Gram. Even though I was instructed not to call Gram or go to her home, I placed a call to her every chance

I got, even just to say "Hi" or "I love you." It warmed me just to hear her voice.

Home life continued to be extremely dysfunctional. Derrick began regularly drinking beer. He and Mom argued and yelled at each other frequently. Eventually, their arguments turned physical, resulting into things being broken in our home. Dad sometimes turned toward me, as though he were going to hurt me, and this always caused Mom to rush between us. She took me with her and we started leaving the house when Dad was drunk. I have many memories of walking the streets of our neighborhood with my mom, waiting for Dad to pass out so we could return home. During these walks, I found it difficult to stop shaking and my legs felt out of my control, making it difficult to walk.

One night when my parents were in a heated argument, Mom was seated on the couch when Dad suddenly leaped from his re-cliner chair. It only took him a few steps to reach her, grabbing her throat with his large hands. She couldn't get away from him. She was pinned in place with her head crammed against the top of the couch. I cried and screamed at Derrick, shouting at him to let her go, but he appeared possessed, as though he couldn't even hear a word I spoke. Mom tried to fight her way out of the vice like grip, but was over-powered by his strength. As I continued yelling, Mom's face changed from her normal, olive tone to a dusky, grayish blue. I knew she was struggling to breathe. The next thing I remember, I held a two-foot tall, thick glass vase over my head, my hands securely gripping the narrow neck. I stood directly behind my father and shouted: "Let go of her! Let go or I will fucking kill you!" I widened my stance, pre-paring to deliver a determined blow. Dad let go immediately and I remember nothing further from that night. Later, Mom told me she had no doubt in her mind I would have hit Dad in the head with the vase to save her life.

❀

Amidst this chaos, I secretly worried that my father wouldn't be satisfied until he took my virginity. I did not want Derrick to be the person to take that from me. In an attempt to have control over my own life and body, I grew determined to have sex with someone else first. Meanwhile, the dynamics with my father had taken a sinister twist: I became the aggressor, approaching him sexually and using all the tricks he taught me. In this way, I could easily manipulate him into doing anything I asked. I felt no guilt or shame; that world had long ago been distorted. Instead, I delighted in my newfound power—a role reversal not at all unusual for children who experience such abuse.

My power-play tactics worked like a charm. Derrick bought wine for me on request; he openly bought my cigarettes and somehow justified it with my mom. He even allowed me to smoke marijuana at home. I started wearing makeup, dressing in the finest clothes, and earned more freedom and privileges. About this time, "sizzlers" became very popular. The silky dresses were cut so short, they came with matching panties. I owned two: one in a solid color and the other with a delicate floral pattern. I wore them with a pair of white "Go-Go" boots. Derrick was surprised Mom allowed me to wear such provocative attire to school.

Most of this escalated during my sophomore year in high school, a year I spent more time out of school than in class. Mom tried driving me to school to ensure my attendance. I promptly exited through the back door. My close friend Cathleen and I spent our day's downtown and I scanned the streets, wondering how I would someday find the man to take my virginity. Cathleen and I enjoyed sitting in a small grill joint, listening to the jukebox, and filling our time with conversation. We smoked a lot of marijuana at that time, experimenting cautiously with other drugs as well.

One afternoon, Cathleen and I went to a house party. Neither one of us knew anyone there, but we were welcomed with open arms. There, I finally found the man I sought, the man who—unbeknownst to him—would save me from giving my father the one thing he wanted more than anything else. I lost my virginity at that party and left with a mixed bag of emotions. The deed itself was insignificant, completely without feeling. I was good at that by then. No fireworks of love, so frequently depicted in the sensual novels, filled my first-time story. No soft words were uttered. I knew I had experienced a tremendous loss—the dream of giving myself to a man I could share the rest of my life with—but the decision was also easy. I had to decide between a complete stranger or my own father. Cathleen and I departed the party and at first I felt a sense of emptiness. Later, I became angry and sad. Acting with a trauma survivor's tendencies, I quickly abolished those feelings and told myself it was the best possible choice given my circumstances.

I'll never forget the day Derrick crossed the line and entered into the act of penetration. Once inside me, without a condom, he lifted his chest off of mine and looked me straight in the eyes.

"You aren't a virgin!" he snapped.

"Nope," I snapped back, conjuring all the sarcasm I could gather.

Derrick stared at me for a few seconds, then resumed the sexual act until he felt satisfied. As he stood beside the bed, he looked down at me once more. I saw anger in his eyes. He had never looked at me that way before and for a moment I was scared.

"I'm telling your mother that you've been out fucking around," he said.

"Go ahead—and I'll tell her exactly what you have been doing to me!" I shouted. With that, I rose from the bed, gathered my clothes, and stomped into the bathroom. Fourteen steps to safety. Fourteen steps to freedom. Except even those blessings seemed lost to me by then. Was I really free? Was there anywhere that I could actually feel safe? When I emerged from the bathroom, Derrick acted as though nothing had happened.

❧

To this day, I feel torn about the physiological feelings of ecstasy that I felt at the hands of my abuser. My mind never doubted that these feelings were wrong. I knew without anyone telling me that I should only experience gratification and satiety with a man that I loved…and that man should never be my own father. Even into my fifties, I fight an internal battle concerning sexual fulfillment. It feels impossible to resolve. But years of reflection and learning have taught me that, although my feelings were my own, they were provoked by something beyond my control. I would never blame someone for being abused at the hands of another. As a survivor, I resolve every day to remind myself that this means I would also never blame myself.

Chapter Five

———— ❀ ————

When I started menstruating, I said the same prayer to God every day: "Please don't let me get pregnant, God. PLEASE." The idea of praying for Derrick to leave me alone was completely beyond my realm of thought. I had experienced years of abuse at his hands. Most days, I completely forgot that another way of living was actually possible. Although I maintained my rebellious streak, Derrick's actions still continued in a vicious cycle of power and abuse. We were locked in. I saw no way out.

Back then, birth control was only available with parental consent. How on earth could a young woman in my circumstances broach that subject with her own mother? *Hey, Ma, I was thinking...since your husband is raping me, could you put me on the pill?* Obviously, this conversation was not an option. I resorted to my trusty power-play as the aggressor, and threatened Derrick with the hope of scaring him into reality.

"What are you gonna do if I get pregnant," I asked. "What would you tell Mom?"

His reply turned my stomach: "I'll talk with her and we can raise the baby," he said. "Together."

I could not comprehend what I had heard. His response rendered me speechless. Soon thereafter, and not surprisingly, I started running away from home. At first, I went to Gram's house but had to stop almost immediately, because my mom always came there looking. When she caught me, she took me home. I was failing every class in school, I shoplifted from department stores, I abused alcohol, and I frequently got high at parties. Perhaps my mom attributed this behavior to "just being a teenager" or "just a phase." To this day, I still do not know precisely what she thought. I do know, however, that she reached her wit's end when she sent me to juvenile detention.

I remember the long, silent drive. I knew exactly where she was taking me. I showed no emotion; no crying, no begging—nothing. I felt scared, but I also felt a sense of peace. Away from home, Derrick wouldn't be able to touch me. I checked in, and the sound of the thick metal door as it closed and locked brought me into my new reality. They had placed me in a room with a small bed, a flat mattress, and a sink. A camera in the upper right corner of the room watched my every move. As per protocol, I was placed on suicide watch for the first forty-eight hours. I cried myself to sleep the first few nights and although I felt relieved to be away from Derrick, I longed powerfully for my mother.

The schedule in the juvenile home was rigid. We woke at 7:00 a.m. to face a row of clean clothes folded neatly on a table in the hallway. I learned to be prompt, getting to the table quickly to find the one pair of jeans that actually fit me. All meals were served on trays in a large room and had to be eaten within a certain timeframe. Permission to go to the bathroom, drink from the drinking fountain, or going to the game room had to be given by a facility monitor beforehand. Failure to do so resulted in the offender being locked in his or her room.

On the second day, I met the counselor. Despite his efforts, I remained silent. Each day I entered the therapy room, sat quietly, refusing to offer a single word. I felt nothing and therefore I had nothing to say. I was unwilling to give any parcel of information. No matter how the counselor posed questions or attempted to carry on simple conversations, I remained silent. After a week, I was not required to attend anymore one-on-one sessions, but I had to be present at group sessions. I sat and listened half-heartedly to other teens describing antics that ultimately led them to juvenile detention but and I felt nothing for them. No empathy, no sadness, and certainly no appreciation for what they may have been through. In my mind, group therapy was an hour of wasted time. I couldn't wait to get out of the room, even if it meant being locked in my own.

In time, I earned privileges based on good behavior. One such privilege was washing and drying the meal trays. This privilege, however, came with a stipulation. If a tray was not thoroughly cleaned, the one responsible had to re-wash every single tray. It was in this kitchen that I first met Mr. B. He was in charge of serving meals, ensuring the cleanliness of the kitchen, and monitoring those of us who had chores. He was an older gentleman who often studied me, although not in a bad way. He was very kind, with a great sense of humor and he never tolerated anyone being disrespectful to him or to others.

One day while I was placing the clean trays in front of him for inspection, Mr. B spoke up.

"Bonnie," he said. "You don't belong here. Have you been meeting with your counselor?"

I nodded my head.

"Are you talking to him?"

I didn't look at him. I only shook my head. Mr. B remained silent.

Every day upon completion of cleaning the trays, Mr. B repeated the same words: "Bonnie, you don't belong here. You are not like the other kids." Every time, I remained silent, offering no expression. But inside, my mind screamed: *I'm strong! I don't need anyone or anything. I don't have to talk if I don't want to!*

❖

I'm not sure if something specific happened or if I just felt like I had endured enough, but one day, I sat on the bed in my small cubicle and stared at the sink. For the first time, I thoroughly examined the thin plastic drinking cup sitting by the faucet. I thought about Derrick going about his usual daily routines: drinking his morning coffee, showering whenever he wanted to without others watching, eating dinner from a plate instead of a tray, and sleeping in a comfortable bed. *Hell, he's out there doing whatever he wants to and I am stuck in here like an animal. I am being punished for nothing! This is not my fault; Derrick is the one who should be treated like an animal—not me. You bastard! I have spent three months in this hellhole, three months away from my Mom, three months without privileges, three months...*

I have no memory of rising from the bed, walking to the sink, or retrieving the cup. But I do remember sitting on the edge of the flat mattress with a fierce desire to tear off a piece of that cup. It took a great deal of effort, but I did. I placed the jagged end of plastic on the soft skin of my left wrist and began a sawing motion—back and forth, back and forth. I applied a little more pressure each time and I didn't feel pain. I didn't cry. I wasn't even angry. For the first time since those few, private moments of peace I had felt in middle school before Derrick's truck pulled into the driveway of our home, I felt tranquility.

I maintained steady pressure on my target and stayed focused, slicing away as though separate from my own body. I could see myself from above, hovering and weightless. The scene looked fascinating and I grew entranced, patiently running the edge of the cup across my skin. My breathing grew slow and steady, as I watched the edge of the cup break through layers of skin. Finally, a small amount of blood rose to the surface and I pressed even harder on the cup. My skin turned red as I continued to work. I was not consciously aware of an actual desire to commit suicide, instead I felt more enamored with the feeling of escape, the idea of breaking the pattern, the blood-red proof that a different way was possible.

Suddenly, the thick metal door opened and startled me. I was quickly subdued by staff members. While some held me down, others completely emptied my room of everything but the mattress and a sheet. They even took my toothbrush. Then—*I was mad.* The long overdue temper tantrum finally arrived. I yelled and screamed as loud as I could, pacing around the small room. As my anger subsided, it gave way to tears. My entire body convulsed uncontrollably, ridding itself of pent up emotions that had long been ignored.

A few days later, I learned that my mom had scheduled a visitation. Due to my attempted suicide, her visitation had been revoked. I felt mentally destroyed. I missed her terribly. The next time Mr. B approached offering his mantra—"Bonnie, you don't belong here. I can't help you unless you talk to me,"—I finally divulged my secret.

The next thing I remember was being released. I felt so happy to see my mom arrive and the first thing I wanted to do was go home. We hugged each other tightly. I didn't want to let go. My mom told me that Derrick had stopped drinking, they were doing well, and he admitted he had taught me how to use a condom. At the time, I felt my confession had been validated, yet I wondered why he had not come clean with the rest of his secrets. While I was curious, my new found freedom of leaving JD and walking the beginning of what I hoped might be a new path was foremost in my mind.

Chapter Six

———— ❀ ————

O nce I returned home, Derrick didn't make any sexual advances towards me. Soon, all my reservations disappeared. For the first time in years, I viewed my family as normal. We went camping, enjoyed trips to other cities, rode on motorcycles, and truly enjoyed each other's company. My Dad and Mom were happy together, no more fighting or arguing. It seemed too good to be true, but I loved being home. I returned to school and did well. However, as Gram and Mom have warned many times: "A leopard never changes its spots." They might have been saying this to warn me of returning to my deviant ways. However, I was not the one who needed to be viewed with caution; what they really should have done was directed their mistrust toward Derrick. It wasn't long before he returned to his abusive behaviors, dragging me back into the fray.

My mother was so happy with Derrick, so vibrant, and I could hardly stand the thought of hurting her. That fast, I began using drugs daily and skipping school. My mother and I barely spoke to one another and my desire for freedom outweighed my loyalty to her. I don't know how many more times Derrick sexually abused me before I left, but eventually the scales tipped. I was *DONE!* I could not stand the thought of him being on top of me ever again. No more dirty pictures, no more oral sex, no more intercourse and no more fear. No matter how scared I felt or how much it might hurt my Mom, I had to go...

I was sixteen years old, a runaway, and a minor. Very quickly, the police became involved. Most of my friends were older, living on their own with husbands or boyfriends. Some had police scanners and I became quite accomplished at outrunning the police in their relentless search. It wasn't long before those that housed me did not want the police knocking on their doors. I was truly on my own with nowhere to turn. I obtained rations from fast food restaurant trash bins. I spend nights walking the streets downtown, reminded of the many walks my mother and I had taken years before, while Derrick calmed down from his drunk. On colder nights, I browsed through various department stores to get a little warmth. If the cold became unbearable, I was always welcomed at my friend Cathleen's.

One night, Cathleen confessed to me that she had a physically abusive ex-husband. When she was 7 months pregnant, he had pushed her down a flight of steps, causing her to miscarry. Naturally, she was devastated and eventually, after years of abuse, they divorced. Cathleen and I shared a common ground, a true understanding of how abuse can change a person's life forever. We accepted each other for who we really were. Through this connection, we established a deepened trust and one night, she offered me speed. Did we realize the path we were embarking on at the time? I don't think that we did. In our short-sighted needs for survival and validation, speed was a quick-fix that felt too good to deny.

It didn't take long for me to enjoy the feeling of being alert, always wanting to be on the move, and staying up for days at a time. I loved being free of worries and traumatic memories. Speed also curbed my appetite and I no longer had to dig through dumpsters for my next meal. I frequented bars where men were willing to buy drinks in endless supply. The hardship of finding a place to sleep was soon diminished, as I discovered having sex with someone meant I had a bed to sleep in each night. Although I didn't know it at the time, I had earned a version of freedom that I thought I longed for. I laughed and enjoyed the company of those around me. In my disillusioned state I believed that no one stared at me, no one judged me, and no one knew my deepest secret. For the first time in my life, I felt a sense of equality. Of course, there was no way this union could last.

Eventually, marijuana and speed didn't provide me with the "all over good feeling" I needed. I tried new drugs—whatever they were, I wanted them. I experimented with blotter acid, yellow sunshine, Crystal T, and Red T; some to swallow, some to snort, and others to mix with marijuana. I spent Friday and Saturday nights at the bar, dancing and drinking. Sporadically, I placed a call to Gram, usually on the rare nights I was unable to sleep at someone's home. She always answered the phone with a sense of urgency in her voice.

"Are you alright Bon? Where are you?"

I assured her I was fine.

"Come here and stay with me and Papa," she often pleaded. "I'll make fried chicken, mashed potatoes and corn. Please Bon, please come here and stay."

But I always declined. I simply could not bear the thought of her seeing what I had become. Her granddaughter was not the same girl she used to love. I was a drug addict, thief, and frequent drinker of alcohol. At a gaunt ninety pounds on a five foot three frame, would she have even recognized me on her own doorstep? I doubted it.

Chapter Seven

———— ❊ ————

On a cool fall night in 1975, I wandered aimlessly along the dimly lit sidewalks of downtown, looking in the windows of department stores. I marveled at mannequins dressed in the latest fashion trends. I wondered if I could ever dress like that, or would I forever wear garage sale, second-hand clothing. I continued walking in front of a jewelry store, tracing my finger along the glass as I gazed at glimmering diamond wedding rings. Each facet twinkled with shades of brilliant blue and lavender and I thought of how lucky a woman would be to receive an item of such beauty and affection. I reached the end of the block and entered a game room to ease the evening chill. I had been to this particular spot before, playing my favorite game called "Pinball Wizard." Under the thick glass of the device was a design depicting Elton John as he walked down the Yellow Brick Road in platform heels.

As I angled for the back of the room in search of Pinball Wizard, I noticed a breathtaking man leaning up against my favorite game. I approached and we quickly engaged in conversation. He was the most handsome man I had ever seen; beautiful hazel eyes and golden brown hair that fell at the top of his shoulders. He donned a perfectly trimmed mustache and sideburns, and the most flirtatious smile imaginable. Joseph and I left the game room together and from that night on, we became inseparable.

As he drove, we never stopped conversing. He explained he was house sitting for a couple who went to Florida every year during the winter. When we reached our destination, I grew speechless. The house was huge, overlooking a frozen, snow-covered lake. The kitchen contained every gadget one could possibly want and others I had never seen before. The living room featured a magnificent, wall-sized picture window, giving way to a beautiful view of the lake as far as the eye could see. Another wall had a massive stone fireplace that offered a sense of warmth. All of the furniture was over-stuffed, totally enveloping those who sat down. To my eyes, this home was perfect. I wondered if the owners appreciated its beauty like I did, or if they simply took it for granted.

Joseph and I stayed there together in this home into mid-spring. We shared everything and I felt we were meant to be a couple, compatible in every way. Joseph was my first love; a love that grew so big, I had previously thought such feelings were impossible. Our young hearts were pure, un-jaded by past experiences of love gone wrong. This deepened our bond, locking us in intense affection without reservation. It became all-consuming. We cooked dinners together, took long walks in the evening, and sat by the fireplace, mesmerized by the flickering fire. We shared our hopes and dreams, as well as sharing the numerous drugs we both enjoyed. I felt sad when we had to leave the house, and I soon realized Joseph didn't have a pot to piss in or a window to throw it out of. But this practicality didn't matter to me; I was still totally in love.

By late spring, I decided Joseph and I had played Russian roulette with unprotected sex long enough. I did not want to have children, so I began taking birth control religiously. Come early summer, I had severe abdominal pain that eventually warranted a trip to the Emergency Room. The doctor informed me I was having a miscarriage and quickly scheduled me for emergency surgery to remove the products of conception. Afterwards, he increased the strength of my pills and assured me I would be fine. I was not convinced.

Three months later, I was pregnant again. During the pregnancy,

I began to see Joseph's true colors. He was a womanizer, a modern day Don Juan. He made no attempt to hide his desires. He dated numerous other women, even while I was pregnant with our child. One day, he even drove to Gram's house with another woman in the car. Gram was mad as a wet hornet. She had come to love Joseph like a son, but she was very angry about how badly he treated me. The once fairy tale relationship, turned quickly into a private hell. For the sake of our child, I was determined to stay with him and try to make it work.

Midway through my pregnancy, mom moved me into her apartment since Joseph and I were in a "on again- off again" relationship. My mom had been divorced for quite some time. Our relationship had been strained for years, but we made co-habitation work. I suppose we had both reached a point in our lives in which we shared a mutual acceptance and respect for one another, despite it all. I saw Joseph infrequently, as he still chased other women. He was keenly aware of my mom's bitterness towards him, not to mention her Italian temper. From time to time Joseph picked me up (most likely in another woman's car) and we went for long drives. I loved him very much, despite his wrong doings, and I never once thought we would be separate from each other in the end.

❖

In 1977, after a mere four-and-a-half hours of labor, I gave birth to the most beautiful baby girl, with my mom and Joseph present. Nyna had a full head of thick, dark black hair and I loved her more than anything in the world. Suddenly, life was all about this beautiful little being who was completely dependent upon me for survival. While some couples plan to have children, others like me are totally unprepared. I was as poor as a church mouse, a high school dropout, and had no income. How would I provide for this little, innocent infant? Our families came together, donating used towels, washcloths, plates, silverware, pots, and pans. Mom purchased a beautiful, white, wicker bassinette and clothes for her granddaughter, and Gram provided sheets, paper towels, toilet paper and canned goods.

Within a month, Joseph and I moved into a two and a half car garage that had been converted into a small, one-bedroom house. It wasn't fancy by any means, but it was a roof over our heads. The dwelling came with a small, apartment-sized refrigerator. Its freezer held four pounds of burger with no room to spare. We also had a stove, a small sink, limited cupboards, and very little counter space. The bathroom was restricted to a shower stall, petite sink and toilet. Joseph's grandmother gave us a bed, mattress, and box springs. Thankfully the bedroom was large enough to accommodate our bed and the baby crib. I had a rocking chair that had belonged to Gram and Grampa, providing the one place to sit in the living room. That was the extent of our décor. We didn't have a television, end tables, or lamps. Thank God we at least had a radio!

I briefly qualified for public assistance, which provided baby formula and a modest amount of groceries. Still, life became a daily struggle. I could only afford to do laundry one time per month and since we didn't have a vehicle, I had to borrow a child's play wagon from a neighbor. I piled all the laundry in, put my daughter on top of the heap, and walked four blocks to and from the laundry mat. We didn't have a chest of drawers, so laundry was placed in two piles on the bedroom floor: one side was clean clothes and the other side was for dirty.

Disposable diapers were a luxury I could not afford. Instead, I used cloth diapers, diaper pins, and plastic pants. I washed those diapers every single day in the kitchen sink by hand and placed them on the clothesline even in the dead of winter! My daughters' daily bathing was done in the sink as well. She loved it though, splashing water all over the small countertop and floor, giggling and playing with plastic spoons. When she was old enough to sit on the floor, her playtime consisted of banging utensils on pots and pans. The louder the noise, the better she liked it. Unfortunately, Joseph missed a lot of his daughters' achievements like rolling over, sitting up independently, and learning to play. He was far too busy spending nights with whoever caught his fancy. Sometimes he came home long enough to change clothes while the flavor of the night before waited in the car parked in our driveway. I always felt inferior to them, as though they were beautiful women with the world and my Joseph at their fingertips. By contrast, I saw myself as mediocre, not at all good-looking or pleasing. I had no self-esteem, no sense of self worth, and had felt substandard since grade school.

❈

When our child was 6 months old, she became quite ill with an upper respiratory infection and fierce cough. I battled her intermittent fevers, poor eating, and inability to rest. As long as I held her up towards my shoulder, she slept for hours. The pediatrician prescribed a cough syrup containing codeine, which I gave her at the exact times indicated on the bottle. Grampa picked me up one evening to take me to the store for juice, as this was the only thing my daughter would readily accept. Joseph happened to be home and stayed behind to babysit.

Upon my return I discovered a terrible, overwhelming odor coming from the oven. I asked Joseph what was in there, and he told me he was cooking marijuana with some of the baby's cough syrup. I flew into an uncontrollable rage. The horrible things he had done to me hit like a ton of bricks: running around with other women, stealing rent money from me, never holding a job, selling my belongings, and now, jeopardizing his own child's health by using her medicine for his drug habit! I kicked Joseph out of the dwelling right then, throwing his clothing and personal items into the yard. As he walked down the driveway to the street, I cried like a baby. I felt alone and petrified, something I had felt profoundly at the hands of Derrick many years before. Everything felt overwhelming and impossible. Sure, I had survived life on the street, but this was different. I had an innocent, little being depending on me but I didn't even have a phone, a car, or a job.

Thankfully, I met the requirements for public assistance and this held us over for a little while. When my benefits ran out, I had to find a job. I was no stranger to bars, as my mom was a great bartender and had owned a pub in the past. I had spent enough time with her throughout the years to learn waitressing and bartending, and that is where I chose to look first. I ended up working three jobs, at three different bars, six days a week, to make ends meet financially. My first shift began at 7:30 a.m., which was a busy time due to factory workers ending their night shifts. The establishment offered a great selection of breakfasts, and once the rush ended, I could clock out around 10:30 or 11:00 a.m. By noon, I clocked in at another tavern, tending bar and waitressing until 5:30 p.m. From there, it was a quick trip home to shower and change clothes for the longest haul of the day, which began at 7:30 p.m. I waitressed at this last watering hole until 2 a.m. and cleaned the pub until 3 a.m. By then, I felt dog-ass tired and couldn't wait to get home for much needed sleep. A generous co-worker always offered to drive me home and I never turned down the opportunity. The hardest part was not having my daughter around, as she spent over ninety percent of her time with a sitter. I hated leaving her, but I couldn't see any other way to pay bills, buy food, and clothe my daughter. I did make good money from tips, which served as cash in case of a minor emergency.

Several months after Joseph and I broke up, I learned more about his secret life. He had been incarcerated numerous times for multiple infractions and not long after we parted company, he was arrested. I chose not to take Nyna to a prison to see her father through a thick glass window, and I never once regretted that decision. As Nyna matured she began to ask questions about her dad, one of which she posed frequently: "Momma, did my dad love you?" My answer was always the same: "Yes Nyna, he loved me as much as he could love anyone." Each time, I answered her questions honestly never making him appear to be better or worse than he was.

❀

In 1980 I met Evan. He was a lead singer/keyboard player in the house band at one of the taverns I worked in. The band played six nights a week and the bar was always packed. Evan was five foot ten, solid as a rock, with a voice that sounded just like Elvis. We talked regularly and soon we moved on to dating. He was thirteen years my senior, owned a nice home, and I suppose I may have seen a sign of stability—something I hadn't experienced in a long time.

Within a few months, I moved into his house along with Nyna, who was three years old. Evan bought me nice clothes and jewelry, opened doors for me, and paraded me around like I was a queen. I felt a warming sense of security. There was always food on the table, a nice bed to sleep in, and a roof over my daughter's head. She had everything she could have possibly wanted. What I didn't realize was that Evan was slowly molding me into what *he* wanted. I had to dress a certain way and talk in a manner that was acceptable to him. I had to tell him when I was leaving, where I was going, who I was with, and when I would return. He also grew quite controlling of Nyna as she grew older, limiting her friends and laying down the law regarding where she could go and how long she could be gone. It wasn't long before I learned that Evan had a long history of assaulting former wives and girlfriends.

One evening, I bravely said to him: "Don't you ever hit me. I watched my mother live that way and I always said I wouldn't tolerate that."

Evan paused for a moment, then looked up at me. "I won't ever hit you honey," he said, and he remained true to his word.

By 1982, our family of three moved into a farmhouse on ten acres of land. Over a period of time we acquired livestock, chickens, and also boarded a few horses for additional income. By this time, Evan

no longer played music but he did dabble in fixing up old farm trac-
tors for re-sale and further cash. He began changing, but not for the
better. He became destructive and had to be in command of every
single thing. He controlled what was to be watched on television,
what would be made for dinner, the décor of the house, what could
be planted and where, when and where I could go, and whom I could
speak to on the phone. I placed the blame on all the hard liquor and
Evan's years of fighting in Vietnam. Still, I knew I would have to
make a major transformation in my life that would enable me to be
in control.

In 1983, I went back to school for my GED. That same year, I
applied for the Nursing program at a local community college. There
was a year-long waiting list and I used the time wisely, completing
all the pre-requisite classes. I had absolutely no previous experience
in nursing but I knew I could do it. During this time, Grampa grew
ill and stayed in a critical care unit. One day while visiting with him,
he made me promise I would finish school.

"I will Grampa," I said.

"Promise me," he said. He looked me in the eyes.

"I promise, Grampa. I will finish school."

He didn't live to see me graduate from the nursing program, but
I did so in 1987. Nyna was 10 years old. Mom, Gram, Nyna, and
Evan were present for the graduation and I already had a job lined
up. I took my state board licensure test and passed; making me a full-
fledged Registered Nurse in the state of Michigan.

It was such a great feeling to get that first paycheck. I had never
made that much money at one time in my entire life. However, Evan
had other plans for my money. Soon, I had only an allowance of my
own paycheck for gas and meals at work. Evan knew exactly how
long it took me to drive home from work. Anything over the time
had to be explained. I felt so torn and confused. I wanted out of
our relationship, but I wanted to be home too. I despised being controlled. Both my mom and Gram were very disappointed in how

Evan treated me, but they let me make my own decisions and readily helped me when I needed them. They were my counselors, listeners, and the rocks that held me together. Little did I know an event was coming and the choice I'd make would haunt me, fostering feelings of grief, anger, and regret for years to come.

Chapter Eight

———— ❀ ————

Nyna was eleven years old that Halloween night in 1988 and we planned to visit numerous stores to trick-or-treat. I told Gram we would stop by for a few minutes, but by the time Nyna and I finished at the mall, it was getting late. Nyna had school the next day. I drove straight home, figuring I could stop by Gram's the next day when Nyna got home from school.

On November 1, I awakened with a start from a deep sleep. I sat straight up in bed, completely overcome with a compelling thought in my head: *Call Gram.* I glanced at the clock. Only 5:00 a.m. *She isn't even up yet.* I lay back on the bed, ignoring the impulse, eventually drifting back to sleep.

Again, I was awakened: *Call Gram.* I looked at the clock: 6:30 a.m. I headed for the phone, muttering to myself, "She must be up having a cup of instant coffee by now." I dialed the number and listened as the other end of the line rang and rang. No answer.

After a few minutes, I dialed the number again. Still, no answer. *She has to be there, she doesn't drive,* I thought, and just like that, a slough of thoughts raced around my mind, faster than a moving freight train: *Maybe she fell trying to take a shower and that's why she isn't answering. Maybe she's pissed off that I didn't stop by last night and she's being stubborn. Maybe her phone is broken.* I paced from one room to another as my heart raced. *O.K., I will call Mom. Maybe she knows what's going on. She lives closer to Gram's house than I do.* I stopped pacing and took a few deep breaths, attempting to gain composure.

"Hello?"

"Hi Mom...it's me, Bon"

"Yes?"

A deafening silence filled the line. I didn't know what to say, and Mom obviously detected something wrong in my voice. She awaited my reply.

"Have you talked to Gram this morning?"

"Noooo...Why?"

"Well, I've tried to call her, but she isn't answering the phone." The deafening silence thickened, threatening to take my breath away.

Finally, Mom replied nervously: "I'll call you right back."

A few seconds later, my phone rang.

"Hello?"

In a voice wracked with anxiety, Mom replied: "She didn't answer. I'm going over."

"O.K., I'm on my way too."

I drove like a bat out of hell, all the while talking out loud: "Gram, if you have fallen trying to shower without help, I'm going to be very upset with you. And if you're not answering the phone because you're mad, I'm really going to be upset with you!" Fear and anxiety overwhelmed me. I fought back tears, hoping Gram was not gone.

"I really hope you're just being stubborn Gram," I continued. "I'll feel better if you have only fallen, and I won't be mad at you...But if I get a damn speeding ticket and find out you're fine, I'm gonna be mad...O.K., well...if a cop tries to stop me, I'm gonna keep driving and, Gram- I won't be mad at you. I promise."

The closer I got to Gram's house, the emptier I felt. I began bargaining with God: "I'm sorry God, I promise I will keep my word, just please let her be fine. I know I have sinned a lot and I have done some horrible things, but please don't take her away from me. PLEASE. I will try harder to be a better person Lord, please let her be alright." As I rounded the last corner toward Gram's house, I saw my mom's car in the driveway. Quickly, I pulled in behind it and turned off the engine. I could only stare at Gram's house. It looked different: hollow, altered, an invisible dark cloud covering the house and yard. The warm, happy place I had known since childhood now felt cold. I knew she was gone.

I don't remember walking up to the door, but when I opened it, I heard Mom sobbing. I halted in the entryway and suddenly I couldn't muster a single step from the threshold. The entire world stopped, the only sound was that of my mother crying. It was the most awful, gut wrenching sound I had ever heard. I entered the kitchen and walked towards the living room. That's when I saw Mom leaning over the hospital bed where Gram lay, ever so still. I dropped into a fetal position on the floor, sobbing, begging my mom to tell me Gram wasn't gone. I pleaded over and over: "Mom, please tell me she isn't gone, please Momma, please." Despite her own pain, my sweet mother sat on the floor, held me in her arms and rocked me back and forth like an infant. Each time I begged her to tell me Gram wasn't gone she spoke: "Honey, I can't tell you that."

At some point, Mom placed a call to the police and then to the funeral home. I finally gathered the courage to walk over to the hospital bed and stroke Gram's face and hair. I picked up a few Kleenexes from her bedside table and stroked her face again. Her skin felt so soft; her beautiful silver hair looked neat as a pin. Gram looked as if she was only sleeping and I felt grateful she got what she always wanted: to die at home in her sleep.

All too quickly, a shiny, clean, black hearse pulled in front of the house. Two tall gentlemen got out, each wearing long black trench coats. As they entered the house, Mom greeted them. I studied the men, noting their clean and polished shoes. They stood in a military-type pose. Both looked clean-shaven with meticulous haircuts, not a single hair out of place. I don't remember if they came in with the gurney, or if they went back out to get it, but I do remember them gently transferring Gram from her hospital bed to theirs for transporting. As they reached for the rails to wheel her out I stopped them, asking for just another minute. The men simultaneously placed their arms behind them, standing perfectly still and made no eye contact. I knew once they left, I would never see her again. There was to be no funeral per Gram's wishes and no visitation.

After they left, I went into the kitchen to sit down. On the counter sat my daughter's Halloween gift. If I had taken the time to stop the night before as I said I would, I could have seen Gram one last time. If I had called her at five o'clock in the morning, maybe I could have heard her voice one last time. But I didn't.

I placed a call to Evan, telling him Gram passed away. Within minutes, he pulled in the driveway. Even though he was obsessively controlling, he did show true compassion and sympathy when Gram died. His concern comforted me and I realized there is a certain amount of good in everyone.

❖

A few weeks after Gram's passing, I remembered a conversation we shared about a sighting I had at work. I told her I was working the night shift one evening and noticed the staff kept the hallways dimly lit to ensure our patients rested well. Each time I came out of a patient's room, I caught a fleeting glimpse of a form wearing a long, black, flowing garment with a hood. Gram asked if I could see the form's face and I told her that it always turned away very quickly and I could not. I do know that the figure seemed to float as it moved, barely touching the floor.

"It is the angel of death, Bon," she told me.

"Well, why is it here with me at work?"

"Someone very close to you is going to die," she answered.

Of course, I had never thought about my own Gram dying. I had always seen her as immortal.

❖

Several months passed before Mom received Gram's death certificate. The time of death shocked me: 5:00 a.m. She had indeed come to me when she passed away. I still felt very angry at God for taking Gram away from me. This feeling lasted for five years. I didn't pray and I refused to talk about Him. My feelings of guilt for not visiting Gram clouded my vision and confused my Faith.

I often had intermittent dreams that took place in Gram's house. I remember feeling a tremendous urgency to speak to her; but she always departed before I uttered a single word. After each dream, I awoke short of breath, perspiring and crying. My heart raced. Time and time again, the outcome of the dream was the same. One night, I dreamt I walked down the hallway and into Gram's kitchen. Gram stood at the sink, her hands immersed in the soapy bubbles. I felt no anxiety or urgency as I had felt during previous dreams.

I stood beside her and calmly spoke: "I love you, Gram."

She turned her head and looked at me, then gently placed her right arm around my waist. "I love you too, Bon."

When I awoke, at long last I felt a deep sense of peace and tranquility. I could feel the intensity of the guilt I had held onto for so long, fade away. I realized I needed to rid myself of blame and enable myself to move on.

I still think of Gram often and I keep a picture of her hanging in my hallway. I can see her hands, her smile, and her beautiful silver hair, all reminding me of good times. I miss her every single day, but I know she watches over me and guides me especially when I feel deeply troubled.

Chapter Nine

❀

By 1990, Evan and I had been celibate for six long years and our connection was very strained. I had stepped out of our relationship and was physically involved with a man from work. I knew beyond the shadow of a doubt if Evan ever discovered this, the outcome would be dreadful. My affair lasted almost two years and the resolution was mutually decided upon. I contented myself to live with Evan, even though it was not an ideal situation. In truth, I couldn't imagine going back to being poor nor did I want my daughter to endure such a radical change. She did well in school and had a group of long time friends that she adored. Providing Nyna with a sense of stability was very important.

It came as a complete surprise when Evan proposed marriage and offered a beautiful diamond ring. I had never imagined he would choose something so binding, especially since he had been married twice before. It was even more astounding that I said yes. Evan chose the date and location for the nuptials and we married soon after, in Las Vegas. We had been together for ten years. Part of me hoped our "new" commitment would improve the relationship. Deep down, I knew it wouldn't. It didn't take long after the "I Do's" before Evan became verbally abusive and domineering. His drinking reeled out of control. I went to work and he sat at the bar, which meant Nyna did her homework there afterschool. I knew better than to question Evan or even suggest that he take her elsewhere. My sixth sense always guarded me and I never totally trusted that Evan would control his anger. Something about him kept me on my toes at all times.

One evening, I lay in my bed with Nyna, talking about the things we had done earlier that day. It was our time to connect before she went to bed. Suddenly, I heard a loud popping noise and quickly recognized it as a gunshot! At first I was stunned, but I was also able to remain as calm as a tree without wind. I felt no fear or anxiety.

I spoke softly to my daughter: "I'm going to see what is going on," I said. "If you hear anything like arguing or fighting, you climb out the window and run as fast as you can to the neighbors."

Nyna nodded her head.

"No matter what you hear," I continued, "keep running and don't look back. O.K.?"

"Yes momma, I will."

"Promise me, my girl" I touched her soft cheeks and locked onto her eyes.

"I promise, Momma."

I gently kissed her on the forehead, got out of bed, and entered the living room. A part of me hoped Evan had shot himself, but there he sat, splayed across his recliner with a 45 caliber gun in his hand. The T.V. had a hole in the screen. The most frightening part of the incident was that the T.V. sat against the same wall as the bedroom! I found it difficult to hide my disappointment that he was alive, let alone my shock that he had been so careless.

"What the hell is wrong with you?" I shouted.

"Well," he said, "Elvis shot his T.V. and I wanted to see how it felt."

I couldn't come up with anything logical to say, so I simply retreated to the bedroom and went back to bed.

Not long after, Evan and I began target practicing with his gun, shooting at a metal coffee can. At first it felt awkward for me, but, in time the gun felt normal in my hand and I became a pretty good markswoman. One afternoon, I hit the target straight on as I had on other occasions and Evan started walking toward the target to reset it. I hadn't shifted positions and the gun now pointed directly at Evan's back. Everything moved in slow motion and I felt my finger was on the trigger, the steadiness of my hand. I thought about the Sherriff that lived directly across the street and how I could claim the shooting was an accident. *"He walked in front of me as I fired the gun,"* I would say. *"I didn't mean to do it. I didn't see him in time."* In an instant, I knew: *It's time to move on, Bon. It's time to get out of here.* I handed Evan the gun, went inside the house, and I never fired the weapon again.

I had left Evan so many times I'd lost track. Each time, my mom would take me in but Nyna always cried and acted out, begging to go home. In 1992, I mustered the strength and courage to leave Evan for the last time. He departed for his "make-shift" job one morning and I acted like everything was normal. I watched as he pulled out of the driveway and when he was out of sight, I made my move. I never knew how long he would stay away, as he came home periodically throughout the day. I had to act quickly. I approached Nyna and calmly gave her clear, precise instructions: "We are leaving. Here are two laundry baskets for you--get what you really want and put it in here. DO NOT lolly-gag around. We have to go."

I took the two family heirloom antique tables, work uniforms, clothes and some knick-knacks and placed them into the bed of the pick-up. I urged Nyna to make her decisions quickly and within thirty minutes we vacated the house. I worried about getting caught, but once I had safely driven out of Evan's normal route I felt relieved. In my haste, I forgot several items of sentimental value and had to return to the house several weeks later. I took Mom with me. I'll never forget what Evan said as I picked up the last item from the deck: "You won't have a thing without me. How dare you stick me with all this debt! I put your ass through school. You'll be nothing more than a gutter slut just like you were when I met you." I turned around to face him and responded: "First of all, you did not put me through school. The government did. And second, I *will* make it."

The truck I had used to make my getaway was also the vehicle Evan had been letting me drive back and forth to work. Soon the game of control began. I hadn't considered Evan might have a spare set of keys, but it soon became apparent. Countless times, I stepped out of Mom's house to get into the truck, only to discover it was gone. By the time I called in to work to advise them that I couldn't be there for my shift, the truck would be returned. The mind games threatened my sanity, but I never doubted my choice to leave.

❦

After several months, I saved enough money to move into a very nice apartment complex in a different city, just ten miles from work. The apartments were brand new and I took one on the main floor with sliding glass doors that opened to a cement patio. The apartment had two bedrooms, two bathrooms, a spacious living room, and a kitchen/dining room, as well as a laundry room. Appliances were included and it even had a dishwasher! I felt like I had finally made it. I was on my own, free to make my own decisions and live life. I bought new furniture for the first time and made the apartment home. I decorated exactly how I wanted to. I watched what I wanted on television and listened to my radio whenever I chose. I was finally divorced, happy, and free.

I should have known Evan would not give up that easily. I worked second shift at a hospital and clocked out at 11:00 p.m. One night, I strolled through the parking lot toward the truck, but the spot had a different vehicle in it. I wandered the brightly lit parking lot searching every row. No luck. But I felt certain I knew my parking spot and when I returned to that row, the truck waited for me, right where I had already looked! I knew beyond the shadow of doubt that Evan had masterminded the trick. He wanted me to know he could take the truck anytime he wanted. At least back in my own apartment, Evan couldn't find me. How very wrong I was!

The first phone call came on my day off, one lazy summer afternoon.

"Hello?" a man's voice said. "I know where you live."

"No you don't," I said. "*Evan.*"

"Oh, but I do," he scowled. "Look out your front door window."

Sure enough, there he stood. I opened the door in a flash.

"Aren't you afraid?" he said.

I stared at him and almost laughed. "Nope," I said, and I shut the door in his face. Of course, I felt profoundly afraid, but my mind rattled along one simple, determined thought: *This is my home and you will not run me out of here. I don't need you; I can make it on my own!*

I began paying more attention during my commute and confirmed that Evan was indeed following me. I knew I was in danger. My mom felt equally afraid for my safety and we both realized the extent of harm Evan was capable of inflicting.

❈

Within six months of my divorce I met Matt. He was everything Evan despised. Matt dressed like a biker with a leather vest, boots, a tri-fold wallet on a chain, and long hair. He didn't have a motorcycle though, or a car. I knew Evan would be disgusted once he knew about Matt and that was my goal. After a few months of dating, Matt and I got engaged and married in 1993. The sole purpose for me was to save my life. Matt moved in with Nyna and I but she absolutely couldn't stand him. They bickered like siblings and drove me crazy. Matt tried to be a dad to a teenager he barely knew, which drove Nyna further away. I was at a point in my life where it was "my way or the highway" and Matt really didn't stand a chance. Neither did our relationship. He was raised to be kind, gentle and polite, often viewing the world through rose-colored glasses. He bowed down to me, always avoiding conflict.

One day, I prepared to go grocery shopping and Matt asked me to buy different toilet paper. Ours wasn't soft enough. I turned around and replied: "Are you kidding? If you want different toilet paper, have your mom get it for you!" The poor man; I refused to budge on anything. No one would tell me what to do ever again. I continued treating him badly and I was consciously aware of my behavior. Matt rolled with the punches and even that began to irritate me. I couldn't bear the thought of having sex with him and I cheated on him while we were married. I disliked the way he dressed, the way he walked, and anything he said or did. I even instigated arguments in an attempt to get him to leave. But Matt stood firm, enduring my horrible actions without reaction.

Eventually, I asked him to move out. I drove him to his parents' home, along with his personal belongings. I left as soon as he unpacked the car, deliberately avoiding his family. I felt no sorrow or guilt for the way I treated him, I just wanted him gone! The divorce was finalized five months after our marriage and I felt relieved. I was on my own again; free to do what I pleased. A few years later, I saw Matt downtown at a festival. He sat in the third row of bleachers, listening to a band. I seized the opportunity and I apologized for the way I treated him. "You came along at the wrong time in my life," I confessed. "You are a good man and I'm sorry for hurting you." I hugged him and walked away.

❀

During the short time I was married to Matt, we visited regularly with his friend named Larry. Larry was a very kind, polite, single man, who was self-employed in a lucrative business. He was in his early thirties and had been married and divorced. We hit it off from the start and began dating as soon as Matt and I divorced. Larry was a romantic man, frequently sending me flowers at work or surprising me with a greeting card and stuffed animal. He had a wonderful sense of humor, childlike and playful. I felt welcomed by his family with open arms and we visited his parents often.

In 1994, Larry and I married and went all out for the occasion. Larry requested I wear a formal white wedding gown but I debated, reminding him of the number of times I had been married. "Well," he said, "it's the first time you're marrying me." I found the perfect gown, loaded with white pearls and sequins. The train had three ornate lace panels outlined with tiny pearls. The hem had a lace ruffle falling perfectly at my feet. I wore white satin flats that provided comfort during the wedding and reception. The bouquet draped to my knees with long tendrils of green, silk ivy as well as purple lilacs, white roses, and white hydrangeas. Pearls cascaded over the flowers. I felt like a princess in a fairy tale wedding.

Several months later, I purchased my first house in the country. Soon it was decorated, offering a calm and charming atmosphere. There were two bedrooms, a modest living room, an open kitchen and dining area, a nice sized bathroom and a full basement with a washer/dryer and recreation room. I was employed by the local hospital just seven miles from home, an added bonus. My first spring there, I designed and implemented flowerbeds. I planted coneflowers, purple delphiniums, a wisteria vine, hybrid two-tone irises, a snowball bush, and a snow fountain weeping cherry tree. The home looked peaceful and beautiful, and I remember thinking: *Gosh, maybe this will be it.*

Larry utilized the large pole barn as his workplace, which was acceptable as we both shared a love for antique cars. He had tremendous talent in restoration but he remained lax about completing his projects. Before I knew it, car parts obstructed my once beautiful surroundings. I became frustrated with his lack of drive in life, as well as constant telephone calls from customers who were less than cordial when they didn't get their goods on time, as promised. Larry displayed a passive demeanor and I reverted to my old aggressive behavior, criticizing his work ethic, lack of zest, and our celibate relationship. Just like my previous relationships, I asked him to move out of our home on numerous occasions. Within a few weeks, I always cried and begged him to return, and he readily accepted.

I used to coach myself: *I can make this work, I know I can.* I even tried being very frank with Larry about what I needed from the relationship, but he made no efforts to change. I remained honest in my communication, yet he refused to engage in discussions. After five years of marriage coupled with multiple break ups and reconciliations, Larry filed for divorce.

I had no desire to sit in the courtroom for our divorce proceedings. Instead, I stayed home and cried as I reflected on my failed relationships. *What is wrong with me? Why do I keep landing in relationships that breakdown? Why is it that the men in my life don't want to have a physical connection with me?* I couldn't make sense of it all. On a whim, I stopped into a counseling center one day and asked to talk with a staff member. Within minutes, a well-dressed middle-aged woman escorted me into her office. She introduced herself and asked why I was there.

Before I could censor my own thoughts, I blurted out: "I was molested by my dad for many years."

Tears flowed immediately and the counselor handed me a tissue. "I'm sorry," she said. "I know how you feel."

I looked up and saw her gaze of pity as she studied me. I felt suddenly enraged. "Have you ever been molested?" I snapped.

"No. No, I haven't."

"Well, then don't sit there and tell me you know how I feel because you don't!"

I left her office abruptly and made up my mind that I didn't need anyone to help me. I had gotten through school, I had saved myself and my daughter from abusive relationships, I had found an apartment and then owned my own home. I had stood my ground, hadn't I? I longed for Gram and her sage advice. I hardened my resolve and dug my heels into my own logic. Of course I could keep going.

Of course I could handle life on my own. Of course, of course, of course...

❈

After my third failed marriage, I experienced frequent episodes of crying, anxiety, and depression. I struggled to concentrate and fought intense fatigue. My temper raged. The smallest obstacles in life sent me on a tear. My family physician prescribed an antidepressant and after four weeks on the prescription, I felt slightly better. My mood swings continued I often felt I had nowhere to turn. Nothing in my life contained elements of peace, quiet, or a sense of ease. Had I ever really felt carefree? What would my daughter remember about the men I brought in and out of her life? What memories would she keep of my temper, my failings? I wanted to provide for her, yet exhaustion crippled me. Someone always needed something from me, even in my work as a nurse, and it had become my mode to oblige. I could feel the life draining out of me. I felt unhappy at home, burnt out in my career, and I had absolutely nothing left to give.

❈

In 2000, I met John. He was a friend of a family member and I saw him frequently at social gatherings. At the time, he was married to an alcoholic who was always on the lookout for one-night stands. John and I spent a lot of time talking about the difficulties in his marriage. He badly wanted to end his relationship. I stood in as his support system, offering a shoulder and advice. By the time he divorced his wife, John and I had known each other for three or four years. Not long after, we began dating. He held a steady job in home health care and seemed very happy with his career. After a year of dating, John asked me to marry him. We went to the courthouse and avoided the alternative of a costly wedding. It certainly wasn't my first go-round with matrimony. I remember standing in front of the judge, my mouth so dry I could barely swallow. I felt as though I couldn't breathe—nothing at all the way a bride should feel. My mind shouted at me to stop the ceremony and run. But that same exhaustion that had crippled me for years kept me rooted to the spot. The relationship was quickly doomed, with my patterns of disgust in my husband and failed attempts at communication quickly taking over. I began another affair. Despite several attempts to save our union, John and I were not able to work through our troubles, and in 2008 I asked for a divorce. Enough was enough. I took one more vow in my life and that was a vow that I would never be in another relationship again.

❧

For the next six months, I buried myself in work. I pulled extra shifts and stayed late. Non-work days quickly filled with housecleaning, yard maintenance, and laundry. I did bi-weekly grocery shopping on Saturdays with my mom and that was the extent of my life. I turned down numerous opportunities to join work buddies for dinner or a cocktail, always using some excuse of having a prior commitment. I was still on my own and owned my own home, but the monetary debt was substantial.

In my mind's eye, I was happy: I had no one to consider but myself. I didn't have to pick up after anyone, I didn't have to tolerate empty promises, and I could do whatever I chose. In reality, I had created a life of solitude. What I perceived as freedom was merely a protected existence. I didn't have to worry about anyone taking anything away from me, nor was I threatened or fearful of being hurt emotionally. I even went so far as to re-decorate five rooms in the house, a task which provided an ironic sense of security. With each brush stroke and strip of wallpaper, I sealed my world up tightly. That world, however small, was a world I had made and it would not be taken away from me.

Chapter Ten

———— ❁ ————

One evening, I received a phone call from Nyna. She wanted me to go the tavern where she worked as a waitress. After her relentless begging, I gave in. The tavern was crammed with customers and I quickly felt uncomfortable. Loud music boomed and I longed to retreat, but before I could turn around, I felt Nyna's arms around me. Her happiness was unmistakable.

"Hi, Ma! I'm so glad you're here!" she shouted over the crowd. "Come sit down at the bar. I'll buy you a margarita."

I took a seat and within seconds Nyna placed a cocktail on a napkin in front of me. She and I talked briefly and it wasn't long before I felt more comfortable. At some point, I met a young woman with a bubbly personality. While Sarah was young enough to be my child, we seemed to have an indescribable bond. By the end of the night, she and I made plans to meet at a local bar and grill to watch Monday night football and have dinner.

When I returned home, I struggled with the thought of the plans I had made. I didn't want to go out into the world again. I didn't want to expose myself emotionally, even to a harmless, kind, young woman. I hated the thought of being in another room full of strangers, strangers who might judge me or see right through my failures and secretive past. I decided that on Monday afternoon I would call Sarah and withdraw from our plans.

Before I knew it, Monday arrived. I got home from work and

rushed to the phone to call Sarah and cancel our plans. A message waited for me on the machine. I pressed play: "Hi Bonnie, this is Sarah. I had some errands to run, so I'll meet you at 8:30, ok? I can't wait to see you! We are going to have such a great time. See ya soon." Panic set in and after much internal debate, I finally decided I had no other choice but to show up. I scurried to gather clothes, checked my make-up and hair, and headed out the door.

When I arrived at the restaurant, I found Sarah sitting on a bench outside the front entrance waiting for me. We took a seat at the bar, ordered our entrees, and engrossed ourselves in the football game. Sarah confided in me about her recent divorce and lack of friends other than mutual pals of her ex. She expressed her joy in finding someone she could spend time with, and in doing so it got her out of house for a few hours a week. Part of me wanted to tell her I felt the same, but getting to the bar had been hard enough. I'd save my feelings for another day. Even still, by the end of the game we agreed to make Monday nights a ritual. To my surprise, I felt good about the decision.

❀

One Thursday night, Nyna called, begging me to come to the bar. "It's dead as hell here ma," she said. "I'm bored out of my mind. Can you come down for a while? Please!" She met me with open arms and a warm smile, quickly making me a margarita. I took a seat at the bar and Nyna joined me. At first, our conversation was about my grandchildren. I wanted to know how they were doing in school and how Nyna felt about her job and boyfriend.

Soon, Nyna changed the subject. "Ma, there is someone I'd like you to meet."

Red flags flared in my brain, a deadly storm approaching. "Nyna, I am not interested," I replied. I looked her in the eyes so she would know how serious I felt.

"But Ma, he's a wonderful guy. I like him so much…and he's single, too."

I laughed and said, "Even more of a reason for me to say no as you and I have the complete opposite taste in men. Besides, I'm really good right now in my life."

"What life, Ma? You work all the time and you go out for dinner on Monday nights," she retorted. Then she looked at me bashfully. "That's not a life, Ma."

"Nyna," I said, "I don't have the energy for another relationship. I don't want nor do I *need* anyone in my life. Besides, I am content right where I am. The answer is no."

Nyna knew she had lost the battle. I finished my drink, gave her a hug and kiss, and promptly left for home.

❖

The next Monday, Sarah and I met for our weekly outing. We had just finished our dinner when two gentlemen walked in, headed straight toward Sara. She knew them well and they exchanged hugs and warm welcomes. Both men were young, perhaps in their early twenties. Sarah introduced us and I replied with a cordial, cool hello. I couldn't help but notice they both sported thick, long beards—something that always repulsed me. Of course, the scruffier of the two took a shining to me.

Conversation flowed easily and I laughed to myself thinking, "Good grief! I'm old enough to be your mother!" When my cell phone rang, I stepped aside and answered, elated to hear Nyna's voice on the other end.

"Hi, Ma. Whatcha doing?

"I'm sitting here with Sarah, watching the game. What are you doing?" I asked.

"Nothing much," she answered with a deep sigh. "How about coming down for a drink, Ma?"

I reiterated that Sarah was with me and Nyna suggested we both come along. Sarah's friends quickly invited themselves along as well and, before I knew it, we were off.

At the tavern, I noticed Nyna sitting on a man's lap at the bar. As soon as she saw me, she jumped down, rounded the bar with her beautiful smile, wrapped her arms around my neck, and thanked me for coming to see her. Then she turned around and headed back towards the man she had sat with moments before. She motioned for me to tag along.

"Mom, this is Thomas. Thomas this is my mom, Bonnie."

I knew immediately what she had done, but I remained polite saying, "It's nice to meet you."

He responded with the same welcoming words. Thomas' lack of interest was as unmistakable as mine, yet I couldn't help noticing his unique, captivating, beautiful eyes. I headed for the table Sarah and her friends had chosen and within minutes, Nyna set a margarita in front of me. The next thing I knew, Nyna was done with her shift for the evening. She suggested that we all head down the block to another watering hole and the decision was unanimous.

Once inside the establishment, Sara took her place at a high-top table with four chairs, her entourage still in tow. I seated myself and ordered a beverage. Mr. Scruffy Beard found it very difficult to keep his desire in check as he pulled up a chair next to mine. Since his behavior wasn't out of hand, I made no attempt to move him. I scanned the room, noting how crowded it was and that's when I spotted the man with the hypnotic eyes again. I looked at Nyna, only half-surprised. Before I said a word, she spoke up.

"Yes, Ma...I knew he was coming here."

"Wonderful," I said sarcastically. Every so often, I turned to look for Thomas, the man with the amazing eyes. As soon as I'd locate him, I returned my attention to the company at my table. Eventually, I mustered the courage (or was it foolishness?) to saunter across the floor towards the back of the room where Thomas leaned against the wall. *What the hell are you doing?* I thought. *It's got to be the alcohol.* But within seconds, Thomas met my stare and there was no stopping me.

"Hello," I said. I felt spellbound by his eyes.

"Hello," he replied. He spoke in monotone. He appeared completely composed as he held my gaze. I, on the other hand, lost total awareness of the activity around us. I simply could not shift my eyes away from his. *If the rest of him is anything like those eyes, I'm going to be in trouble,* I thought to myself. Then it happened, like something out of a Humphrey Bogart movie where he and a woman are engrossed in the moment and he presents a romantic question that leaves viewers in awe.

Without shifting his gaze, Thomas asked, "You want to kiss me don't you?"

"Yes," I said. "Yes. I believe I do."

That kiss was like no other I had ever experienced. It expressed everything I needed to know. Passionate. Gentle, yet firm. Overflowing with immeasurable feeling.

The next thing I knew Nyna, and I were heading to a restaurant for a meal, following Thomas who was ahead of us in his vehicle. I'm not able to remember if she and I even spoke as I drove. When we arrived, we sat at a round table, placed our orders and before I knew it, I sat on Thomas's lap. We kissed like love struck teenagers.

Looking back on that evening, I can only imagine the impression other patrons must have had, but, at the time, I couldn't get enough of Thomas. I didn't get home until well after four in the morning. When my head rested on my pillow, I sighed and then smiled, replaying the night's events. I pictured Thomas' thick dark hair, beautiful eyes, strong hands, slender 5' 10" frame, and the breathtaking kisses we shared.

That's when the logic set in. Quickly, I constructed walls to restrict whatever might happen next. These were the kinds of walls I've relied on for most of my life. I could have built them with my eyes closed. These walls offer me a sense of safety and provide a sense of control. *Bonnie, you don't want another relationship remember?* The walls seemed to whisper. *Thomas will be fun to play with for a minute, but that's it! That is where it has to stop. He's just for entertainment, nothing more!* I drifted off to sleep, restless and uneasy.

Before I opened my eyes the next afternoon, visions of Thomas flashed through my mind as if from a motion picture. I knew I wanted to see him again. I went to the tavern to see Nyna, but secretly hoped I might also see Thomas. I nearly gave up, then he strolled through the door. We smiled at one another as he spoke my mind: "I was hoping you would be here."

❀

From then on we spent as much time together as we could. My once mundane, solitary life was suddenly filled with excitement, anticipation, and nightly outings. I admired Thomas' enthusiasm for life, his ability to completely take charge in a crowded room with his animated antics, as well as his serious side. People were drawn to him like a magnet. His circle of friends was substantial and nearly everyone had been a part of his life for many years—something I had never known. Thomas also demonstrated a sense of self-confidence and a high degree of intelligence along with his easy going, gentle disposition. He was self-employed in the business of auto body repair and paint, and was highly respected by his peers and customers. *How ironic* I thought. *Another car enthusiast.*

Thomas and I had been dating for a few months when I stopped by his shop on an unannounced, quick visit. An older woman sat inside waiting for her vehicle to be fixed. She spoke softly to her black dog. I took a seat across from her and politely said hello. She looked at me and conveyed the same greeting, and I knew immediately the woman was Thomas' mother. Her eyes were the mirror image of Thomas'—the same unique color and just as captivating. I liked her instantly. Engaging in conversation seemed natural and very comfortable, as though I had known her for years. Thomas joined us, introduced me to his Mom, and seemed pleased that she and I had been talking. When I left for home, her face and mannerisms remained in my mind. I remember thinking: *It's no wonder he is such a gentleman—opening doors for me, addressing others as Sir and Ma'am... and his strong work ethics. She taught him how to be a man.*

One afternoon, we made the decision to move in together.

"You know my friend Ron?" Thomas asked.

I nodded.

"Well, he has to find a place to live with his family and he suggested renting my house." The words hung like balloons. "Ron thought you and I could move in together, and I think it would be a good idea."

My stomach flipped and my breath stuck between my mouth and lungs. In an instant, my mouth felt dry and my brain flooded with thoughts, both positive and negative. The pause in the discussion was obvious. Thomas waited for a response; one that I couldn't seem to select, as there were so many things to consider. The logical side of my brain recognized the fact that Thomas was at my home more than his, but this proposal would add an element of finality and could quite possibly end in failure. I'd already experienced so many unsuccessful relationships in my life. The willy-nilly side of my brain offered a different perspective, leaning heavily towards accepting the proposition.

"O.K.," I said. I wanted to feel joyful, but instead felt all too aware of the fear that totally enveloped me.

Chapter Eleven

* * *

It took a few months for us to meld together. After all, Thomas had been single for quite some time following a hostile divorce. I certainly had my share of walls to tear down, too. Nevertheless, we adjusted to one another's habits, working out the kinks and differences until we became comfortable. We discussed mistakes we had made in our previous marriages and implemented a few rules in order to keep our relationship strong. These are the tips we came up with: never stop dating, never go to bed angry, always be honest, and if either of us wanted out—just say so. The guidelines seemed reasonable and we both agreed to be mindful of our well-chosen directives. One simple pleasure we often shared was having coffee together in the morning while discussing our plans for the day ahead. We never parted company without saying "I love you. Have a good day."

After five months of dating, Thomas' mother became ill, resulting in numerous visits to the emergency room at a local hospital. More times than not, she was admitted for a few days and then sent home as her condition improved. Without hesitation, Thomas assumed the responsibility of her care as well as the upkeep of her home. He ensured her bills were paid, did the grocery shopping, cooking, and laundry along with housecleaning and yard maintenance. He spent the rest of his time trying to keep his business successful and this added pressure yielded frustration. Virtually overnight, he had become responsible for two full-time responsibilities that could not be maintained without his constant vigilance.

Eventually, Thomas moved in with his mom. Our relationship began to bend under the tremendous pile of constant worry, pressure, and tension. Our physical intimacy also suffered. We tried to make time for one another but the sentiments felt forced. I worried about how much weight we could carry before circumstances pushed us apart. However, the Lord above stepped in as if to say, *"No. This is not what I have in mind for you. You WILL make it!"*

❊

Thomas suggested that we take a trip to Florida on his motorcycle to visit a family member he had not seen in many years. The trip was over eleven hundred miles one way. Riding on two wheels and taking the back roads was remarkable. It's amazing how much of the countryside, small towns, and mountains are missed when travelers choose an automobile and the highway as their primary transportation and route. In Tennessee, as we rode through the mountains we caught a glimpse of a storm at the top of a peak, yet it was dry where we rode. When we reached a certain point, water ran forcefully down the mountain, creating the most beautiful waterfall. Small rays of sun glistened against the wet rocks and rain cascaded across the road. It was the most exquisite scene I had ever laid my eyes on, and I will carry the memory forever. Later, as we rode through Georgia, we came upon a barbeque contest in a small park. Smoky, sweet aromas filled the air as we passed slowly from one end of town to the other. Adults and children of all ages took part in the festivities and I thought about how fortunate we were to have witnessed so many people having a wonderful time.

Weather presented the biggest challenge on our journey. It rained almost the entire time, both ways. But if I had it to do again, I wouldn't change one thing—not even the downpours. The ride presented the break we needed to recharge and spend much-needed time together. Thomas kept in contact with the happenings back home on a daily basis, ensuring all was well and, for the most part our, ten-day expedition was void of all emergent situations. Knowing what I know now, the excursion was put into place as a means to get us through the next phase.

As Thomas' mom's health continued to decline, he sought help from home health agencies to assist with her personal care, and eventually she required a hospital bed and visiting nurse services to sustain her physical needs. Her arthritic pain skyrocketed and her bed-bound status caused swelling and intense aching in every joint of her body. I supported and respected Thomas for the love and devotion he showed for his mom, and for keeping his promise to her that he would never put her in a nursing home. I lent a hand when I was able, but I too had a full time job, one that was far stricter in regards to accountability. I had to be present on my scheduled days.

The constant worry took a toll on Thomas, yet he never backed away from the responsibility of caring for his mother. Months passed and he became distant with me. We argued often over what I considered to be silly issues. Eventually, the tension gave way to anger and annoyance in which the slightest obstacle set Thomas into a rage. On one occasion, he didn't speak to me for days over a very minor issue. While it hurt me, I understood wholeheartedly the strain he was carrying every minute of every day and never once begrudged him.

Thomas and I had been together for ten months. On the day of his mom's passing I sat by his side, which meant a great deal to me. Together, we got through her funeral and legal matters. By our first anniversary as a couple, we reunited under the same roof. Thomas was not the same man who had moved out several months before, but I still loved him. He appeared physically and mentally fatigued, his face drawn and his zest for life vanished. In the company of friends, he behaved like his familiar self, but once out of their view he rapidly slipped back into his life of darkness. He confessed to me that on the morning of his mother's passing, she asked him not to leave and he explained his need to go to work. A few hours after his departure, she was gone. He felt she was angry with him for taking off, and it bothered him greatly. I reminded Thomas that his mom had done that almost every time he attempted to leave the house, but he still felt guilty. I easily related to his guilt, remembering when Gram passed. His guilt was not justified. He had cared for his mom in every single way. He remained present whenever possible, assuming all tasks. He also kept every promise.

Even though Thomas and I worked on restoring our relationship, I continued to feel distant from him. We went through the motions, but experienced very little passion. Sentiments that had always come easily, suddenly felt forced and detached. The tension between us felt thick and at times we barely spoke to one another. I faced yet another celibate relationship and quickly chose the path I knew best, reconstructing the solid walls of my fortress. I picked Thomas apart in my mind, ridiculing and criticizing him, just as I had done most of my life in situations that made me feel out of control.

❧

I knew I wanted Thomas to move out but, for the first time, I wasn't able to say the words. I felt aware that Thomas knew exactly what I was considering; still, he didn't budge an inch. One evening as I walked through the kitchen, I stopped and placed my arm on the counter as if to brace myself. I bowed my head and took a deep breath, mindful of how history attempted to repeat itself. A war raged in my mind: *How many times are you going to do this, Bonnie? How many times? When are you going to stop?* I placed the palms of my hands upward and as I looked at them I thought: *You have it all at your fingertips and everything is falling through them, like tiny grains of sand.* I closed my eyes tightly; I had never felt so torn.

I continued leaning against the counter, seeking clarity. I questioned my own intentions: *Bonnie, what is it about this man that keeps you from uttering those irreversible words? What keeps you from turning a blind eye and running?* In a flash, I thought of Gram and I knew without a doubt that Thomas reminded me of her—her trust, her faithfulness, her quiet wisdom, her grace and her unconditional love. I steadied myself and along with it, my resolve. I would not let history repeat itself. I would not keep building those walls. Whatever Thomas and I faced, I felt certain we would do it together.

❧

Months passed and Thomas and I continued co-existing under the same roof however, our behaviors changed. I used to feel a sense of comfort snuggling up to him at night, often falling asleep with my head on his chest. We used to entangle our legs during slumber, always needing to touch in some way. Instead, I found myself hugging the edge of the mattress. Despite my love for him, I still felt conflicted and scared. At times, I wanted to be as far away from him as possible. Other times, I wanted to scream out loud just to release some of the anger I held in. Each time, I stayed my course. Each time, I remember my Gram and the essence of her wisdom, her presence.

Eventually, I had an epiphany. I repeatedly covered up my feelings of being hurt by becoming angry. In return, the anger enabled me to shut down and that allowed me to distance myself. *I* was the one creating the distance. *I* was the one forcing people out of my life. *I* was the one who, despite her best efforts and heart's desires, still put up walls. From inside my self-made fortress, I could shut anyone out in a matter of seconds, like flipping a light switch. I had never cut Mom or Gram out though, despite it all. It must have been that kernel of their character that I sensed in Thomas, too, because I never gave in to the war in my mind and asked him to leave.

At that time, the Lord intervened with a plan. It involved Ron, the man who rented Thomas' home. Ron had made a decision to move out, opting for a larger dwelling. This enabled Thomas to move back into his home. We both felt relief, knowing we needed time away from one another even though we quite honestly wanted to spend the rest of our lives together. The morning after Thomas moved back into his own home, I woke up alone and walked into my bathroom. I looked in the mirror, tasseled my hair, and brushed my teeth. I walked down the hallway into the dining room and then into the kitchen. I poured my first cup of coffee, added my favorite flavored creamer, and lifted myself up on the counter, taking my usual seat. When I looked across the kitchen, Thomas was not sitting there with his own cup, waiting to talk about our daily plans. That's when the tears began to flow. Every room in the house seemed bigger. The warm ambiance was gone leaving a coolness in its place.

It took several days before I fell into a routine, but even that didn't ease the emptiness in my heart. A significant part of me was missing; the other half of my soul departed. I felt very afraid. I felt uneasy at the thought of living alone again, but I coached myself into accepting the new arrangement: *You've done this before Bonnie, and you can do it again; It always comes down to this doesn't it? The outcome never turns out to be what you envision in the beginning, but you have always made it. You can do this again.* Beyond that, however, I worried if Thomas would find peace and contentment without me. I wanted him to be happy in his life, but I also wanted to share my life with him. What if he never comes back?

At first I visited Thomas frequently, making trips across town to his house. Sometimes, we cooked dinner together. Other times, we sat and talked about our lives. After a while I stopped taking the initiative, hoping Thomas would attempt to spend quality time with me. He came around, but the times were few and far between. I became accustomed to the lengthy separations and the infrequent phone calls. Deep down, I hurt every single day. When the opportunity presented itself, I asked Thomas if he ever planned to come home. "Of course I do, baby," he told me. "I'm going to finish the house, put it on the market, and when it sells I'll come back home." More than three years later, Thomas' house is nowhere near marketable and it seems as though other tasks frequently limit his availability to delve into the project.

I had also hoped the distance between us would reignite Thomas' desire for physical intimacy. That part of our life ended abruptly after his mom passed away and I couldn't understand why. I often made flirtatious gestures or hints, but Thomas' actions spoke volumes. He clearly wasn't interested. When we did sleep together, I felt guarded, afraid I might touch him in a manner he found uncomfortable. Over time I became frustrated and internalized his lack of interest by judging myself and my appearance.

❖

Years passed and I slipped back to my old ways, covering the hurt with anger. I contemplated cutting ties with Thomas, but then imagined how awful I might feel without him in my life. I also thought about Gram, and how that sliver of her remained in Thomas. There was and always would be something I could never let go of in that man. Emotionally, I felt I was on a teeter-totter, always moving up and down, yet never really going anywhere. History came knocking again as my depression spread into tearful outbursts and mood swings. I picked up extra shifts at work to occupy my time and chose solitude at home rather than going out with friends. Loneliness engrossed me and I felt I had absolutely no control in my personal life.

The box of secrets I had kept for so long started consuming my existence. Without the outside world to distract me, the tightness of my world was unyielding. If I stayed hidden, maybe no one would ever force my secret out of me. But if I tried to meet the world again, I might have to show my weakness. I might have to face my darkest, most timid, damaged self. The thought terrified me to the point of nearly blocking out the past, but of course, it never loses its weight and hold entirely. The box wobbled and teetered in my mind, encasing me in doubt and loneliness. Some days, it seemed as though the box had a mind of its own, attempting to expose its contents. When

I listened closely, I could hear my younger self, fighting for her life: *Please Dad, please don't make me do this. I don't want to.* Her hands shook and her begging continued. *Why doesn't he hear me? Please God, please help me.* I pictured the little blonde-haired green-eyed girl, crying and begging her own father to stop abusing her. That girl is small and frail, helpless; certainly not a match for the six-foot tall man who became her abuser. The girl could only comply with his demands and eventually stopped begging, seeking control in whatever twisted way she could. Still, her methods were not enough. The rape commenced. Oh, and that girl, that petite, delicate girl...is ME.

Chapter Twelve

I sat in the driver's seat of my car in a nearly empty parking lot, staring at the light tan brick exterior of a building. My thoughts raced, two brains bartering with each other. One cheered me on, arguing for healing: *Three times is the charm Bonnie, you can do this. You are a strong woman now! You are no longer that vulnerable girl. Your father will never touch you again. This building can be your safe place, the place you begin to heal.* The other side played on my fears: *You've tried this crap before and it hasn't worked. No one can help you. Besides, why do think you need help? You are an adult with a successful career; you have a home, a grown child, and two grandchildren. Why dig up the past?*

Then I thought about Thomas, my wonderful, strong, yet gentle man. I considered how close I had come to letting history repeat itself that day that I leaned into the counter, almost kicking him out of my life. While our relationship in two separate homes hadn't been easy, it still provided me with some measure of support and love. I knew Thomas loved me and, more than that, his love was the driving force in my openness to making a change. Without him and without the opportunities that his presence presented me with, I never would have torn down my walls. I never would have contemplated that box. God stepped into my life with a man who reminded me of everything beautiful and strong I had ever known in life. More than once, God refused to let me cast that man aside. Now, it was my job to answer the call: *Get your ass out of the car, march up those steps, and take the first strides in healing.*

I entered the waiting room, breathless.

"May I help you?" a woman asked.

"Yes ma'am" I replied. "I would like to speak with a counselor please."

"Alright" she said softly. "Take a seat and I will be back with you shortly."

The waiting room was empty, yet I chose a seat off to one side and closest to the exit door. I looked around, noticing numerous chairs, tables, and the bright magenta walls. I wanted to run like hell, but I forced myself to remain in the chair by remembering my desire to be a healthy partner to the only man I found worthy of love and trust. Within a few minutes, a woman called my name and escorted me to an office. We sat facing one another.

"What brings you here today, Bonnie? How may I help you?"

Words flew from my mouth, a thousand tiny birds released from the box inside, taking flight all at once. "I was molested by my step father as a child," I said. "I was molested and I need help."

The rest of the visit was a blur, except for the card the counselor gave me with a date and time to return.

❧

The days went by quickly and, before I knew it, my appointment day arrived. I felt nervous before the visit. Part of me wanted to stay home, but the reasonable part of my mind finally stood its ground. I approached the window in the waiting room, gave my name, and took a seat. By the time I completed the two sheets of paper I had been given to fill out, a young, slender, dark-haired woman called my name and escorted me to her office. *Great,* I thought sarcastically, *she's young enough to be my daughter!* I couldn't help liking her though, as she was very soft spoken with a wonderful sense of humor and she had a way about her that made me feel comfortable. My counselor, Amber, kept her office nicely decorated with a small couch, two chairs and two end tables, a lamp, and her desk. In addition, there was a strategically placed box of Kleenex. I hated crying in front of people because it made me feel out of control in front of someone, a feeling I never grew accustomed to.

During one session, Amber and I discussed sex and she asked if I was present during intercourse with Thomas. I laughed and said, "Of course I am." I took the word "present" literally, however, that is not what Amber meant. It wasn't until later that I reflected on her question, uncovering a definite truth: No, I was not present during love-making. In fact, I detached so thoroughly during sex that my mind often travelled elsewhere. I could become aroused during foreplay, but my brain and my body separated during intercourse.

By working with Amber, I made another discovery: I don't reach orgasm unless it is by external stimulation. I dug deeper and realized the time frame in which this dysfunction came about. I had orgasms with my abuser and with Joseph, two men I loved very much but who also caused me great pain. Since them, I had never orgasmed during penetration. The experiences with Derrick and Joseph caused me to lose self-confidence, my ability to trust, and my sense of self worth. In every relationship, whenever I felt threatened in some way, I abruptly cut off all ties as to protect myself from further despair. I had even faked sexual satiety over the years, justifying my actions because I didn't want my partners to feel incapable. In all honesty, I didn't want those partners to recognize *my* inadequacy. Once I faced that mind-boggling concept, I felt the need to reveal my secret to Thomas.

The opportunity presented itself during a telephone conversation one evening, when Thomas inquired how my appointment had gone with Amber earlier that day. Word by word, heartbeat by heartbeat, I divulged my private deception to Thomas. I wanted to be completely honest about every aspect of my life. I finally felt ready to let the committed, sincere, trustworthy partner I knew I could be, meet the world. Thomas' welcoming arms were a wonderful place to start.

Epilogue

— ❁ —

I have remained in therapy for two years and I continue to see Amber regularly. I have been blessed with a therapist I can trust with the most delicate and painful events of my upbringing. She has provided me with tools to aide my healing process. I now know that not everything bad is my fault. There will always be triggers that make me uncomfortable or fearful, but the man responsible can never touch me or hurt me again. During my journey, I have opened the impermeable tomb-like box. I have come face to face with the reality of betrayal and being controlled, as well as numerous failed relationships. I've taken a walk through my life as a victim of rape and a homeless teen, and examined my self- destructive activities with drugs and alcohol.

I am a victim. I always will be a victim. But I am also a survivor because I have a true understanding of the behaviors that often go hand-in-hand with abused children and I work hard to live fearlessly and engage with the world anyway. Behaviors such as dissociation, sexual dysfunction, lack of self-esteem, the inability to engage in social events, feelings of powerlessness and inferiority are a lot to manage, but I feel empowered to do so. Throughout my healing, I have revisited my past and shared my life story, embracing the pleasant and dreadful memories. I have shed a million tears, laughed at the hilarious moments, and experienced tremendous anger concerning my abuse. That once-secret, hidden box has been converted into a toolbox with the right tool for every situation I may encounter. The only person who can hold me back is myself. Knowing this, I vow to always treat myself kindly and respectfully, advancing through life with bravery and focus.

❁

Recently someone asked: "Have you thrown away the dark box that for many, many years, held all of your pain and sorrow?"

After a brief moment, I answered. "No, I'm not throwing it away. I have chosen to decorate it with rhinestones, purple ribbons, and bright colors. It has a new purpose; to hold an abundance of pleasant memories and methods for survival as I venture forward with my family and the one man who is my other half. I am thrilled to see what is yet to come."

Thank You for taking this walk with me for in doing so, I found **ME**! I now have a love for myself, and a sense of self respect and self worth.

My prayer for you is to discover the *REAL you!* Push forward no matter what obstacles fall in front of you, because we are worthy of the very best life has to offer. The walk begins with a single step! GOD BLESS YOU.

Acknowledgments

I am deeply indebted to my family for their unwavering support in my endeavor to reach as many sexual assault victims as possible, with one goal in mind; to help them find their way back.

To my mother Orlena, thank you for always believing in me, and encouraging me to follow my dreams, no matter how farfetched they may have seemed. Thank you for your guidance and love.

To my daughter Nyna, I hope I will always be an inspiration to you. Do not settle for easy, take the hard road and always reach for the stars. You will be an inspiration one day to my grandchildren.

To Thomas, thank you for accepting me for who I was. Somehow you saw something special in me, when I couldn't see it myself. Despite my quirkiness, you haven't thrown in the towel. I thank you now for accepting me for who I am. Thankfully, the clock is still broken.

Special thanks to Gram and Grampa for loving me, showing me how to trust, how to overcome obstacles, and to believe good things come along in God's time. I miss you both every day. I know you are smiling from heaven, proud of the woman I have become.

About the Author

B. J. Parker has been a nurse for twenty-six years. She is a mother and grandmother. Parker lives in Michigan. This is her debut book.

bjParker2014@yahoo.com